Kevin Trudeau's Free Money™

"They" Don't Want You to Know About

Kevin Trudeau's Free Money™

"They" Don't Want You to Know About

Contents

Note To Readers

I'm not a guru, a wizard, or a magician; I'm no financial expert, lawyer, or accountant; and I'm not a butcher, a baker, or a candle-stick maker.

I am the guy who wants you to know that there is free money available to you from government sources—and lots of other places, too. I want you to know that you have the ability to access this free money. Many of the "tricks" of free money are as easy as picking up the phone, or going online, or filling out a form. There are many tips and techniques for you to get cash in your pocket now.

As with any information of this type, it always evolves. The data that I have as we print this book may become out of date tomorrow. That is the way of the world with addresses and website links. Offices move and some foundations do not last forever. But the ideas are not out of date, and they do extend to infinity (and beyond).

We have made every effort to ensure that the information printed here is accurate and up to date, but as in all things in life, there are no guarantees. Time does not stand still. I don't want you to stand still either. I want you to take the wealth of information in this book and apply it!

Find out for yourself how amazing it is to receive free money! If you come across new sources, I'll look forward to hearing about them, and I look forward to your success!

Introduction

Free money.

I'll say it again. FREE money. Maybe you need to hear it this way: Free MONEY. That's right. I said FREE MONEY!

My Mission

This little known and little understood idea of FREE MONEY is a topic that has become almost like a mission for me. When I first started on the "crusade" to blow the lid off the corporate and government shenanigans, I had no idea the course my life would take. In fact, I never intended any kind of crusade at all.

In my books, all of them, I have simply stated what was going on. And what exactly is going on? In a nutshell, the government and the corporate executives want to run our country — at your expense — and they don't like being exposed for what they are doing and what is really going on behind the scenes.

The more I do this, the more I learn, and the more I want to share with you. Somebody has to! YOU need to know what THEY are up to!

They Don't Want You to Know

If you have read any of my prior books, you will know that it ain't pretty. And if you have read *Debt Cures That They Don't Want You to Know About,* you will know that THE FEDERAL GOVERNMENT and the banking executives and the CEOs of the big credit card companies are all in bed together and their common lust is greed.

Debt Cures has sold over a million copies because it revealed all the corrupt and abusive behavior of the people with the power. I blew their dirty dealings wide open and I also revealed probably the most important secret that they don't want you to know about: YOU really are the one with the power!

Knowledge is power, baby, and that's what you get when you read a Kevin Trudeau book. And with this book you hold right now, you will get a whole lot more than knowledge. You can get free money!

> The banks and the companies would prefer to keep you in the dark.

One of the things that I learned during the research for *Debt Cures* is the amazing amount of free money that is out there to be had. And what is equally amazing is that no one knows about it!

Why doesn't anybody know about it? Because they don't want you to know!

Take the Knowledge and the Cash

They don't want you to have it. The banks and the companies would prefer to keep you in the dark. They don't want to give it up. They like ignorant consumers. They like people who take a licking and don't care why it was dished out. They like people who accept the status quo and don't question anything.

That is absolutely not me. I have never accepted the status quo and I question everything. So should you.

It is my curiosity that has launched these information-packed books that have become my life; and truthfully, my curiosity has gotten me into a lot of hot water. Whenever I expose an organization or a group from any business sector or the government, I catch heat. And because I have evolved into the country's leading consumer advocate, I catch a whole lotta heat. And I wouldn't have it any other way.

Obviously, I have struck a nerve with my books. That to me means that I am telling the truth. And they don't want the truth to be told. Why? Because it is a power struggle. They want the power and they want to keep you down and trampled, feeling like you don't have any power and will never have any power.

That is not the case, my friends.

You've Got the Power

YOU do have the power. The power comes from knowledge and that is what I deliver. That is my mission, my crusade. There is so much B.S. (pardon my coarse language) being shoveled at us every day from every direction that I have taken on the job of being a different kind of shovel.

I admit that I get mad sometimes. They attack me. They sue me. They send the IRS hounds down upon me. But I have learned that the secret is to not get mad. The secret is to get even. And how do you do that? Learn what they do and beat them at their own game. That is the secret to my success. And yours.

The beauty of *Debt Cures* is in knowing what the feds and big creditors are doing and how they do it. When you know what you are up against, you know how to play your cards and how to apply the proper strategy. And it works!

I have testimonial after testimonial telling me it works! And that is how my career has become what it is: "Kevin Trudeau, leading consumer advocate and most hated man in corporate America." As long as you are telling me that this information is helping you, I will continue to provide you with the information that you need to make your life better. That is the real American dream. We can have wealth without greed. We can bring back the old-fashioned notion of helping out your neighbor.

Howdy, neighbor. I'm here to help.

They want to steal your livelihood and your spirit and line their pockets with gold at your expense. I say: No way! They — the ones who think that they are the only ones in the know — need to share the wealth.

Get Your Fair Share

There is nothing wrong with wanting your fair share. Armed with knowledge, you can get it. Knowledge is power. And what you are holding in your hands right now is power. The power to get yourself some FREE MONEY!

I call this book *Kevin Trudeau's Free Money That They Don't Want You to Know About* because that has become my trademark line and it's the truth. They don't want you to know about it. There are billions of dollars — give me a neon flashing sign here: BILLIONS OF DOLLARS — and they want to keep their money-grubbing fingers clamped on it.

It is ridiculous! The money is there and belongs to the taxpayers, the hard working citizens of the United States of America. That's right. I mean YOU!

There are so many ways to get a hold of free money. They would prefer that you don't learn these ways so they don't have to pay it out, and I say too bad for them. In the research for the *Debt Cures* books, I have become aware of so many sources for free money. It seems like every day, someone from staff or a reader alerts me to another way or method to find some quick and easy cash.

> The money is there and belongs to the taxpayers

Easy and It Works

And these methods work! I kid you not! There are so many ways that we decided the Free Money chapters in *Debt Cures* were getting too big and bulky and deserved their own book. Wow! An entire book on Free Money! And here it is!

✔ Do you have to be "low income" to qualify? Nope.

✔ Do you have to be a minority to qualify? Nope.

✔ Do you have to be a student to qualify? Nope.

✔ Do you have to be a senior citizen to qualify? Nope.

✔ Do you have to be a farmer to qualify? Nope.

Certainly, there are grants and programs for all of those groups, but I do not fit in any of those categories and I GOT FREE MONEY!

Yes, yours truly applied these methods and ch-ching, some free money was available for me!

✔ Am I low income? Nope.

✔ Am I a minority? Nope.

✔ Am I a student? Nope.

✔ Am I a senior citizen? Nope.

✔ Am I farmer? Nope.

I am a wealthy, middle-aged white male, living in a city, and I used ways that I will talk about here in the following pages, and I landed some free money of my own. It was quick, simple, and as easy as click-click-click.

Knowledge is power. I say that all the time. And now knowledge can also mean free money for you and your loved ones.

The Time Is Now

There has never been a better time for folks to get excited about that!

It is mind blowing. There is money just waiting to be collected. MILLIONS of people qualify! All of the categories that I mention above certainly have the opportunity for free money (low income, minorities, students, senior citizens, farmers) and any other category that you can think of as well.

Are you a woman? Ch-ching!

Are you a small business owner? Ch-ching!

Are you an average, hardworking go-to-work-every-day-to-pay-the-bills kind of person? Guess what? Ch-ching for you too!

Maybe you are a single parent, struggling to make ends meet. Maybe you are doing just fine financially. It does not matter. If you qualify for free money, take it! It is there for you and all you have to do is know where to find it.

That's where this book comes in.

My team is dedicated to the mission I unwittingly started, and this mission has become Free Money. All you need to know is right here at your fingertips. All the reams of research and information have been condensed and distilled, and are ready to be applied.

That is the beauty of this book. Ease of use. My three favorite words. (I also like "Kevin Trudeau Rocks.")

I Like It Simple

Seriously, I am all about keeping it simple for you. No one has time in their crazy hectic lives to sift through volumes and volumes of fine print. We have done that for you. There is the famous free money guy running around out there with his suit covered in question marks and he sells a lot of books. Maybe you have seen him on TV. He is a good guy. I am not knocking him. He is doing a service as well. But if you have ever looked at those books, it can be a little overwhelming. Yes, there are government grants out there and he will list them all. All. It is kind of like reading the phone book.

My approach is a little different. Concise and easy to navigate is my style. Each chapter provides a way to land some free money. Maybe you have money in a long forgotten bank account. We'll tell you how to find it. Maybe you have United States saving bonds that you can cash in for cold hard cash. We'll tell you how to do that. Maybe you have tax money due you. We'll tell you how to go about finding that.

Step by step by step. These methods are not brain surgery. Not rocket science. Not rocket surgery. Believe me, if I can do it, you can too. Frankly, many of these methods are absolutely simple, quick, and easy.

BILLIONS Available

The billions of dollars in government grants (yes, that is correct, *billions of dollars* in government grants) are laid out as well. Finding them is not as tricky as you may think. Fill out a form, maybe a couple of pages, and free money could be on its way to you. I will break down how to do it.

Chapter by chapter, step by step. Free money. Free money. Free money.

(By the way, I am already looking forward to your success stories!)

But back to business. Maybe you are interested in free legal services. We have a chapter on that. How about free dental, medical, or prescriptions? We have a chapter on that. How to get free money out of your house? We talk about that, too.

Flip through and see the topics and how you can walk through and be on your way to free money. No thick book with tiny print to scare you. It's all right here, and we have tried to keep it simple.

I think maybe the other guy wears a suit with question marks because people have a lot of questions for him. I want to give you answers. I want you to get free money. If I were the gimmicky type, maybe I would wear a suit with dollar signs.

No Gimmicks

But that's not me. My "gimmick" is information. My "trademark" is knowledge; knowledge that gives you power.

The government and the powers-that-be have held court for long enough. It is time to take back what is rightfully yours, and what better way than to grab hold of some free money? In these crazy economic times, everyone — and I mean everyone — wants something to hold on to. We all like to hold on to money.

This money that I am talking about is rightfully yours. You are entitled to it! So take it! If you were at the mall and you bought a jacket that was supposed to be 25% off and the sales clerk did not ring it up correctly, you would ask for the 25% discount. You would ask for that cash back. It is rightfully yours. You are entitled to it.

There could be free money sources and methods in this book that you are not aware of. There could be money out there that you should have received long ago. It is rightfully yours. You are entitled to it. Or maybe there are grants or other sources that you qualify for. I repeat: The money is rightfully yours. You are entitled to it.

I'm a broken record so it will get lodged into your brain.

Fill Your Plate

I imagine a big buffet table. There are several silver covered dishes. All you have to do is lift the lid to see what is in there. Each chapter is kind of like that. An item at the buffet table. Maybe it appeals to you, maybe it does not. But if it does, by all means, sample. This buffet is all you can take.

If you subscribe to magazines, many include a recipe or two. All of those recipes are tested before they print them in the magazine for you. They try the recipe to make sure it works and make sure the food tastes good. We sort of did that with *Free Money* in a sense.

As I mentioned earlier, when my team and I started discussing this book, we did some of our own testing. I quickly and easily did one method and ch-ching, a couple hundred bucks for Kevin Trudeau. Very cool.

Did I stop there? Of course not. This is an all-you-can-eat buffet.

I tried something else. Ch-ching. Another $1500 for me.

What I am saying is to go through this buffet line of free money options and try them out. Just because you get money from one source does not mean you are done. Try another chapter. Does it appeal to you? Does it apply to you?

Not everything will. I don't know anyone who goes through a buffet line and takes from every single dish provided. The idea of a buffet is that there is something for everyone, not everything for everyone. But if you do get something from every single chapter of this book, I certainly want to hear about it!

Get Excited!

I get excited about all my projects, but I have to admit, I am really excited about this one! I know that times are tough, and a little extra cash is even more welcome right now. But even in times of plenty, this money is yours. Take it!

If you dropped a twenty-dollar bill out of your wallet, you wouldn't just let it blow away. It is your money. You are the rightful person to hold that twenty, so you would have no qualms getting it back into your wallet.

Think of this free money out there as your money. You need to get it back into your wallet. They — the big dogs — have sat on it long enough. Its rightful home is with you. Are you ready to claim it?

Let's get to it.

CHAPTER 1

Free Money for All of Us

Where do we begin?

There are approximately 4,000 government programs, both federal and state as well as local programs. And these programs give away billions and billions and billions and billions of dollars to people that apply and ask for them.

Magic Word? APPLY!

There are also thousands of independent private organizations and sources of money that go to individuals, too. Now, the secret here is not really a secret. It is common sense. The only people that get the money are those that ask for the money.

Magic word? APPLY! (I told you, I'm a broken record.)

In 2008, 20 million people got free money from some of these sources. But guess what? MILLIONS MORE QUALIFY.

And that is why we are here today. Are you among the millions that are entitled to some of this free money? Odds are that yes, indeed you are.

If I was able to get some free money, don't you think you can too?

The heads are nodding. The excitement is in the air. There are many ways to get your due and that is the game plan here. To tell you where and how. Sound interesting? I thought you might be willing to lend me your ear.

Congress and your senators and your representatives pass bills that include little tidbits in them. It's a big messy game for them. Each guy works it like, "I will say okay to pass this bill, BUT I will throw a sentence into the bill that says I get blahblahblah."

The bill becomes full of blah blah blah.

So Joe Blow Senator will vote yes because his people in his district back home will get money for his various grants.

The kicker is that the people back home in his district have no clue that such grants exist. Kind of a head scratcher. Joe Blow Senator will be able to say that he passed legislation granting home repairs for his people or scholarships or what have you. He will get bragging rights even if no one ever claims the money. Or he lets his friends, family, and fellow cronies know about the stuff in these bills so they can get the money. He just doesn't broadcast it to the rest of us, me, you, and the good people of his constituency.

Get Yours

If you are eligible for that money, don't you want to know about it? Of course you do! Well, ta-da! Welcome to *KT's Free Money They Don't Want You to Know About*. Instead of a flashy suit with dollar signs, I think I will wear a superhero cape instead. (In case you were wondering, that was a joke.)

These bills are monster pieces of paperwork. Thicker than *War and Peace* and thicker than any telephone book. Big, fat reams of paper that no one reads. I have no desire to take the time to read that kind of stuff and I doubt you do either.

This little book is your filter. All the information from those bills and those other books has been poured through a sieve and only what you need to know has been captured. Instead of making you read bills, bills, bills, or lengthy listings of grants, we have produced a streamlined way to get to the money.

This is a ton of information in a portable take-along package.

Quick.

Simple.

Easy.

Yeah, go ahead and sigh. I just did.

We live in a sound bite society. Our mentality is: Just tell me what I need to know. This is your "need to know." This is a ton of information in a portable take-along package.

Quick Ways to Free Money

Do you want to read through all the thousands of government programs and try to figure out what may apply to you? Or do you want to be able to sort first and then read? Yeah, I thought so. The sorting has been done, the simplifying has been done. This Free Money book saves you time, thus saves you money. And also gives you money opportunities. Talk about a dream come true. Pinch me. I love making dreams come true.

Besides this book, there is one other tool you need. The Internet. The almighty Internet. What a beautiful thing it can be when used productively. I applied an online technique that we will get to soon here, and in thirty seconds, I discovered I had $256 in free money for me. Thirty seconds. Two hundred and fifty bucks. I would say that is good use of time.

Some free money is money due you that you don't know about, and some free money is grants and programs that give you money that you don't have to pay back. No matter where it comes from, free money is free money.

Millions Are Entitled!

Millions of people are entitled to this free money. Millions of people. Billions of dollars. I feel like a matchmaker and it feels pretty good.

It blows my mind how much money is just sitting there and how many people have no clue. That is why I have to get the information out there. And new sources and new grants are popping up all the time. That is why I plan on doing a monthly FREE MONEY newsletter as well, to keep you current on the opportunities out there.

This book is the culmination of months of research and gathering of information. As we go to print, who knows what the guys in Washington are up to. I can't hold off publishing this book. This information needs to get into your hands, now more than ever. But rest assured that when new information comes to me, I will get it out to you. I hope you have already signed up for the monthly newsletters, but if not, call customer service now and get on the mailing list. This kind of information is ever evolving, and you want to stay on top of what is new and what is applicable to you and your situation.

So why does it have to be so complicated? That is how Washington operates. But not me. Simple is my specialty. However, the words "Congress" and "simple" usually do not go together in the same sentence.

There has been much in the news with the new presidential administration in office now about budgets and the whole budget process. You probably hear the words earmarks and pork quite often.

Pork

The extra stuff that gets put in a bill is usually called pork. Lately the word earmark has taken over. This senator guy says he will vote yes for the bill if you throw in some money for home repairs for his people back in his state. Earmark. This senator gal says she will vote yes for the bill if you throw in money for education dollars for her people back in her state. Earmark. And so it goes. Every person adds a little something and the thing gets so bulky, you would not believe.

These earmarks don't always get advertised to the folks who could benefit from them, however. Maybe there is money earmarked for home repairs for your state or county or city, and you have no idea. That is why there is so much unspent government money!

Millions qualify, but they don't know about it!

I was reading an article online from CNNMoney.com as recent as March 2009 about the whole scuttlebutt involving debate on the big spending bill. $410 billion on the table. We say those numbers without batting an eye. I repeat. $410 billion on the table. $7.7 billion in earmarks.

Those earmarks are only about 2% of the entire bill, but holy cow, nearly $8 billion in extra stuff that got stuck in the bill as it made its way around Capitol Hill. It is a classic case of "I'll give you this if you give me that."

This CNN report stated, "Typically, when Congress appropriates federal funding to government agencies, it's up to the agencies to decide how that money gets doled out to projects in states, cities and counties, and those decisions are made through an application-and-review process.

"Except when earmarks are involved."

Earmark Epidemic

Yeah. Those earmarks are like a silent pact among thugs. Some wheeling and dealing has always existed, since the beginning of time. At least since the beginning of politics. But the pork spending or use of earmarks has increased tremendously in the past decade. Our boys in Washington like playing games and don't know when to quit.

> Use of earmarks has increased tremendously in the past decade.

This same article explains: "While there have always been earmarks, their number grew exponentially between 1995 and 2006. That's partly because lawmakers began to use earmarks as a way to help incumbents who risked losing re-election. And part of it was a feedback loop: as earmarks grew, so did the ranks of lobbyists to secure them."

"More earmarks begat more lobbyists begat more earmarks." Amen.

President Barack Obama commented about earmarks, "done right, earmarks give legislators the opportunity to direct federal money to worthy projects that benefit people in their district."

But our legislators can sometimes be far from pure in their intent. "On occasion, earmarks have been used as a vehicle for waste, fraud and abuse. Projects have been inserted at the eleventh hour, without review, and sometimes without merit."

If you are a news junkie and want to read the entire article I refer to, please do. See money.cnn.com/2009/03/11/news/economy/earmark_primer/index.htm?postversion=2009031111.

Dear Mr. President...

Part of what President Obama proposes is that earmarks never be traded for political favors. Oh, if only we all lived in a world of candy canes and sugar plum fairies. As long as there are politicians, there will be trading for political favors.

Many Americans are in the dark about earmarks and what goes on in Washington. And maybe you don't care. The point is that there is money to be had and the idea is to make the best use of these earmarks.

So get in that buffet line, and dish up some pork on your plate. (And if you are vegetarian, I am just talking the talk here. You know what I mean.)

I can talk on and on about the bad boys in Washington and their budget busting ways, but the goal of this book is free money, so enough of me talking. There is free money out there, lots of it, so let's get you to it!

CHAPTER 2

US Savings Bonds

The federal government has all types of money for us. They've got it, but do you hear them advertising that fact? Nope. A lot of what goes on in government is kept quiet, but there is no reason that money that is available and due the taxpaying citizens of this country should be kept hush-hush.

If you have money coming to you, wouldn't you want to know about it? Of course you do. But since no one else is telling you, I am. And the plain and simple truth is that you have to be proactive and go after it yourself. That's the beauty of this little book. I will tell you how to do just that.

Do You Have Bonds?

Many people have United States savings bonds that they have long forgotten about. Maybe your grandmother had some years ago. Maybe your parents took some out for you when you were a kid. Maybe you bought some yourself and they simply have been lost.

It is easy to misplace or forget about bonds. They are purchased and then tucked away, waiting for the maturity date when they can be cashed in. In the course of this book, I have asked friends if they have savings bonds. Most get a puzzled look and their eyes roll around in their heads as they try to recall if they have bonds and where those bonds might be.

One pal, Roger, knows he used to have them. In the early days of his career, he was a government employee and he had money taken out of each paycheck to buy bonds. It was an easy and simple savings plan for him.

Roger remembers cashing most of them in when he bought his first house, but he scratches his head at my question. "Now that you mention it, I remember that some of them were not at maturity yet so I could not cash them in. But for the life of me, I cannot think of where they might be."

Roger is not alone. Many, many folks don't know if they still have outstanding matured bonds. Do you want to know if you fall in that category? My first free money step is fun and easy. I love it!

Fast Cash From the Feds!

To see if you have matured bonds that have not been redeemed, check this out.

For easy to read info, go to www.unclaimedassets.com. There was $12.5 billion in value of unclaimed savings bonds as of 2005. As of March 2009, the US Savings Bond Search page says that the amount is now over $15 billion. $15 billion!

That $15 billion is comprised of about 35 million bonds. Are you the holder of any those 35 million?

Bonds stop earning interest after forty years, but they are sitting there, waiting for their rightful owner to show up. People were gifted bonds or used their payroll deduction plans or just bought them outright. More than 55 million Americans have, or had, bonds.

Most government offices simply don't have the manpower — or the motivation — to track down the missing bond owners. They make the case that their records are over thirty years old, and people have moved, changed addresses, been married or divorced so names change. The truth is that there are many reasons why they do not contact people who own bonds, and there are many reasons why bond owners do not realize they have this pot of money sitting there waiting for them.

> More than 55 million Americans have, or had, bonds.

Lost?

The Bureau of Public Debt also makes the statement: "In addition to lost, destroyed and forgotten savings bonds, each year thousands of new savings bonds and bond interest payments go undelivered when the savings bond owner moves and fails to provide a forwarding address. The US Treasury also has billions of dollars in outstanding bearer and registered securities (i.e., Treasury bonds and notes), as well as Postal Savings System Bonds and Postal Savings Notes (Freedom Shares)." [www.unclaimedassets.com/US1.htm]

Every year, over 25,000 bonds and bond interest payments go undelivered because of incorrect addresses. Odds are great that some of you reading this book are in that 25,000 or the 55 million that own bonds.

If you ever want to research any kind of topic like this, you can always start with Google. Type in US Savings Bonds. Go with the extensions ".gov" first. They are the government websites. You can use the aforementioned unclaimed assets website and enter your information to find out if you are in the bond database. Some sites like this charge a small fee.

Always shop around for the site that does not charge a search fee. The website www.savingsbonds.gov will take you to Treasury Direct, a free site. On this site, you will see three columns: One for individuals, one for institutions, and one for government. The last topic listed for individuals is "Check to see if you own matured savings bonds." Give it a click. You may need to scroll down the page until you see "Start Search." Click again.

You can simply enter your social security number or the SSN of the person who may have unredeemed bonds. Instantly you will be told if there is anything in their system for that number. And there is no database search fee.

Search Party

They tell you up front that the database is not perfect. What government database would be?

- ✔ Treasury Hunt does not contain a record of all savings bonds. This system only provides information on Series E bonds issued in 1974 and after.

- ✔ Treasury Hunt may not completely identify any/all savings bonds you may have lost…only those that have reached final maturity and were issued in 1974 and after.

- ✔ Savings bonds returned to Treasury as undeliverable since 1996 can be found by searching this system.

✔ Most records for registered Treasury notes and bonds can be searched through this system.

✔ Also, please note that to file a claim for lost bonds, you must submit a Form PD F 1048, Claim for Lost, Stolen or Destroyed United States Savings Bonds, with information about dates of purchase, names on bonds, and other pertinent information.

[www.savingsbonds.gov/indiv/tools/tools_treasuryhunt.htm]

Any forms you want are available for download, or they will mail to you. They are very short and even simpler to fill out.

Even if the database does not go back to the beginning of time, this is a cool site to play around on. They offer savings bond calculators and wizards. With the turbulent economy, people are again looking for stable "sure things" and savings bonds fit that mold. If you want to see how savings bonds can add up and at what rate, punch in some numbers and let the calculators do their thing.

Story Time

Maybe you do not want to bother with bonds now, but has this whetted your appetite for free "found" money? How about a story from ABC News?

There is found money to be had! A gal named Barbara followed these steps (what "steps"? Providing your name and social security number! That is not too difficult, is it?!) and she landed a big check! Barbara got $2,800 from a bond she received as a gift years ago. The bond had a face value of $500 and when she cashed it in, she was thrilled at the amount she received.

$2,800 in found money from the feds and it did not cost her a penny.

That is all I need to hear to get me going! I hope it gets your blood pumping, too.

Go online or get PD Form 1048 now! Ch-ching!

CHAPTER 3

Bank Accounts

There is nothing better than finding lost money. Ever put on a jacket that you haven't worn in months and found a twenty dollar bill in the pocket? Perks your whole day up, doesn't it? Finding a wad of twenties would be even better.

You just learned that finding old US savings bonds is easy peasy. How about old forgotten bank accounts?

Memory Bank?

Maybe you had a bank account set up by your folks when you were a kid. Maybe Grandma gave you an account when you were in college. Maybe you had an account when you were just starting in the work world or as a newlywed or starting a family.

People move. People change jobs. People get divorced. People go through a journey called life, and along the way, bank accounts are opened and sometimes forgotten. If you had fifty grand in an account, you probably won't forget it, but some of the smaller ones can fall off our radar when life circumstances change.

A bank may consider an account as inactive if you do not make a deposit or a withdrawal within a certain number of months. Some banks will consider the account abandoned if you have no activity within one year.

There is also the unwelcome event that the bank has closed its doors, and as we have seen, that has happened too often lately. Be aware, just because the bank closed, it does not mean that your account is lost forever. Maybe the FDIC issued the funds at the time the bank closed. If not, the money would have been transferred to another bank or custodian account that was set up. These accounts are searchable as well.

Unclaimed Assets

> There are tips for searching for your unclaimed assets.

There are tips for searching for your unclaimed assets. Like I mentioned in the previous chapter, if you are looking for US savings bonds, you have to search the savings bond database. There is no one-stop shopping, no one huge database that houses all sources of possible money that you could lay claim to. Maybe we should invent that. Or maybe there is one that is pretty close. I will get to that in a minute.

When you are searching these systems, be smart. You need to use every advantage, which means you should list all names by which you have been known.

- ✔ Current name
- ✔ Maiden name
- ✔ Previous married names
- ✔ Middle names
- ✔ Initials
- ✔ Nicknames
- ✔ Common misspellings of your name
- ✔ Jr or Sr

You get the idea. Maybe your name is Walter Edward Johnson, but you have always gone by Edward Johnson. Or maybe W. Edward Johnson. Or whatever. Use any and all combinations that could be attached to money in your name.

You should also search every state that you have lived in or worked in, and those of your relatives who may have opened an account for you. There are also accounts often set up in New York and Delaware banks.

Yep, crazy as it sounds, you could have money in states that you never even thought about. Every state (and good old Washington, D.C.) maintains their own system and database for this stash of unclaimed cash. Millions of people have this missing cash out there with their names on it, and they simply don't know to ask for it.

ASK FOR IT!

How? Let me tell you. Let your fingers do the walking.

One option is the unclaimed assets site. I like how this site explains things and how easy it is to get around. Try it yourself at www.unclaimed.com/lost_bank_account.htm. My only misgiving is that they charge a small fee to do the search for lost bank or credit union accounts.

If I can avoid a fee, you know I do. So let me tell you about the National Association of Unclaimed Property Administrators, or NAUPA. I kid you not.

Remember I mentioned the desire for a one-place-has-it-all kind of search tool? This is about as close as we are going to get, and let me tell you, the getting is good. To see for yourself, go to www.missingmoney.com.

This website strives to include as many sources of money and property as humanly possible. The site is updated monthly and it is FREE to use. To get started, the first screen has a space to enter your name and state. Click.

Yep, money. Money, money, money.

FOUND MONEY!

Results appear immediately. The information box identifies the state the money is held in, the last known address, the company or holder of the money, and the amount — either more than $100, less than $100, or unknown. How cool is that?!

You can search under your name, a family name, or the name of a business. If you are the business owner, you can claim the money. If it is your name, of course you can claim the money. (Duh.) If the money is in the name of a family member and you are a legal heir, you can claim the money.

I swear this is the fastest magic I have ever seen to find your lost money! Less than thirty seconds and I discovered I had money due me! My friends are all trying this fabulous method and the results are stunning. Even if you get fifty bucks, like one friend Nick, don't you still want that fifty bucks? You bet you do!

Any money that is rightfully yours, you should lay claim to. If you want to give it to charity once you receive it, that is your business. Do with it what you will. Just do it! Lay your hands on this lost treasure now found!

I am well aware that some people out there are skeptical. Try it! Any agency or company that owes you money is probably in this database. They are continually updating and it gets updated each month.

The NAUPA people also link to state unclaimed property pages if you do not find your missing money here, and they also have "other links" that take you to federal agencies. I am not blowing smoke here. *The Wall Street Journal* has reported that there is nearly $33 billion of unclaimed cash and property sitting in the coffers of state governments. Wow! It could be yours. It could belong to your deceased relatives, which means it could be yours. It could be from an old business of yours, which means it could be yours.

> ...nearly $33 billion of unclaimed cash and property...

If you find a match, you have to file a claim to collect the money. The directions are right on the site. Basically, you have to fill out a form for the state and provide identification that you are the person owed that money. The state will then process your claim and send you a check. Usually you do not know the exact amount until the check arrives. That can be a sweet surprise!

It's free to use the site. What are you waiting for? Go on. Give it a whirl. I'll be waiting for you in the next chapter when you are ready. Good luck!

CHAPTER 4

FOUND Money!

Welcome back! I bet many of you are shaking your heads in amazement. I bet many of you found some lost money! I want to hear about it!

Possibilities...

And if you played around on the website, you discovered that there is so much more out there than just forgotten bank accounts. Are the wheels in your head turning now? Think of all the possibilities:

- ✔ Safe deposit boxes
- ✔ Stocks, bond, mutual funds, dividends
- ✔ CDs
- ✔ Uncashed checks and wages
- ✔ Escrow accounts
- ✔ Trust funds
- ✔ Insurance policies
- ✔ Deposits with utility companies

The database at www.missingmoney.com has those gorgeous golden eggs, too. It's a beautiful thing.

I take these facts about unclaimed property from the folks at NAUPA (www.unclaimed.org/what/):

- ✔ Every U.S. state; District of Columbia; Puerto Rico; the U.S. Virgin Islands; and Quebec, British Columbia, and Alberta in Canada have unclaimed property programs.

- ✔ Unclaimed property laws have been around since at least the 1940s, but have become much broader and more enforced in the last 15 years. Unclaimed property is one of the original consumer protection programs.

- ✔ $1.75 billion was returned to the rightful owners in Fiscal Year 2006 from 1.9 million accounts.

- ✔ At least $32.8 billion is currently being safeguarded by state treasurers and other agencies for 117 million accounts.

- ✔ Claims can be made into perpetuity in most cases — even by heirs.

- ✔ $4.686 billion was received in FY 2006 from business accounts where contact with the owners has been lost.

Do you know that word perpetuity? All it means is that in most cases, there is no deadline to lay claim to the money. If the property is yours, it is perpetually yours and you have the right to it.

The National Association for Unclaimed Property Administrators totally rocks. They say what I want to explain to you, so I will let them say it:

What is unclaimed property?

"Unclaimed property" (sometimes referred to as "abandoned property") refers to accounts in financial institutions and companies that have had no activity generated or contact with the owner for one year or a longer period. Common forms of unclaimed property include savings or checking accounts, stocks, uncashed dividends or payroll checks, refunds, traveler's checks, trust distributions, unredeemed money orders or gift certificates (in some states), insurance payments or refunds and life insurance policies, annuities, certificates of deposit, customer overpayments, utility security deposits, mineral royalty payments, and contents of safe deposit boxes. [www.unclaimed.org/what/]

Each state has laws that protect you, the consumer, and prevent the company or bank from taking over your money. It is yours, plain and simple. They, the business owners, are required to turn over the money or property to the state authorized official who becomes the keeper of the lost loot.

> Each state has laws that protect you...

If the lost loot is stuff and not money, states do not have the capacity or storage facilities to hang on to this stuff forever. What they do is hold auctions and the money received for your item is then held for you.

Do You Have Lost Loot?

States, so I am told, do actively try to find the rightful owners of the dough. Maybe, maybe not. All I know is that they work with NAUPA to update the www.missingmoney.com database. That, my friends, can literally mean money in the bank for you.

And I quote: "All the information is accessible free of charge by searching the state databases or MissingMoney, or by contacting any state unclaimed property office." There will always be someone wanting to charge you for what you can get for free. It does not mean that you should pay it.

All of this information that I share with you is free and available at your fingertips. See www.unclaimed.org for all that NAUPA has to offer.

Maybe you have found free money thanks to NAUPA and www. missingmoney.com. Congratulations! Now you may be thinking about how to avoid missing money again in the future. NAUPA has that covered, too:

> You should contact institutions that hold your money or property every year and especially when there is an address change or change in marital status. For security reasons, most financial institutions do not forward mail. Keep accurate financial records and record all insurance policies, bank account numbers with bank names and addresses, types of accounts, stock certificates, and rent and utility deposits.

> ✔ Cash all checks for dividends, wages, and insurance settlements without delay.

> ✔ Respond to requests for confirmation of account balances and stockholder proxies.

> ✔ If you have a safe deposit box, record its number, bank name and address, and give the extra key to a trusted person.

> ✔ Finally, prepare and file a will detailing the disposition of your assets.

> [www.unclaimed.org/what/]

Are you having fun playing around on this site? Uncovering any lost treasures? Be sure to tell your friends and family members about this amazing resource. There are countless numbers of people who could benefit from learning about this site.

Missing Money Found

If you need some real life stories, I have them. MSNBC reported in March 2009 that California has $5 billion in unclaimed cash. One man, George of San Jose, used this fabulous website and found $5,800 of his money! In these tough economic times, or anytime, that is a lot of cash! (Source: www.msnbc.msn.com/id/29453405/)

The state of Oregon has $250 million in their treasure chest of unclaimed money. The Department of State spokesperson says that one in four Oregon residents have money in that chest. The state of Washington collected $100 million in unclaimed loot in 2008.

The news reporter who reported the story on the unclaimed assets in Oregon and Washington used the unclaimed.org website and discovered that she had free money waiting for her, too! She has more than $100 coming from her university in Boston. There's no better substantiation for a news story than that. (Source: www.kcprtv.com/news/40753757.html)

> The state of Washington collected $100 million in unclaimed loot in 2008.

The state of South Carolina wants to find you and give you back your money. They have a program called the Palmetto Payback that actively searches for the owners of abandoned accounts and unclaimed property.

In 2008, they gave back over $12 million. Wow. Now that's one government program I can applaud. The largest payout to date to one individual is over $76,000! Holy Carolina! (Source: www. scnow.com/scp/news/local/article/state_wants_to_rid_itself_of_ unclaimed_property/29864/) Now if that amount doesn't motivate you to do a little digging for your own found money, I don't know what will! I have more stories, but I think you get the idea. Now, are you ready to get busy?

> When I learn about such remarkable resources, I want to get the word out.

This is fantastic stuff! Now I think you can understand why we wanted to do this book. When I learn about such remarkable resources, I want to get the word out. There are so many ways to get free money into your life, and the effort is so minimal! Who wouldn't want to give it a try?!

Let me know how you do!

FDIC

And maybe you have been going through the records of your deceased relatives and you came across bank statements from banks that are long gone. Contact the FDIC (Federal Deposit Insurance Corporation) for help in tracing the history of a bank you know nothing about. They have a toll-free consumer hotline that you can call with any questions: 877-ASK-FDIC (275-3342). Their website is www2.fdic.gov/funds/index.asp.

If an account is more than ten years old the funds are probably lumped in with unclaimed property at the state treasurer's office. So besides everything I have told you so far (NAUPA search database, etc.), each state can be contacted.

Most people don't realize that states have unclaimed property offices. Why don't you know? All together now: They don't want you to know!

But lo and behold, my research team has done the work for you. In Appendix I, we have listed the contact information for all the states. When you locate property that you think is yours or your relative's funds, you have to fill out a claim form. To request a claim form, you have to go through the state in which the property is held.

Escheat

I don't want to complicate the issue, I just need to explain something. When talking about unclaimed property, you may come across the word "escheat." That is the legal word for the process that allows transfers of unclaimed property — from banks, credit unions, stock brokers, utility companies, employers, life insurance companies, and all the other places that may end up with money and stuff that goes unclaimed — to a government holding trust.

If you see the word escheat or an office or agency with that title, you know you are in the right place.

All of the money from all of those above-named places is sitting and waiting for you to come claim it. Billions of dollars. A tiny fraction gets back to its rightful owner.

So many more areas we will tackle, too, as we go:

✔ Veterans Benefits

✔ Life Insurance

✔ Gift Cards and Certificates

The ideas are probably bouncing around in your head. I hope so. Be alert and be aware to all the possible free money and found money avenues out there.

Family members are often unaware that they are entitled to collect the unclaimed cash and property and benefits of their deceased relatives. Many people die without detailed or organized financial records, so their heirs have no idea. Many people also die with no will or an outdated will.

Take a piece of advice and make sure your will is always up to date and keep records of your assets and holdings. Let someone close to you know where to find your records in the event of your death.

One in three life insurance policies are not claimed. Can you imagine? Family members do not know that the policy exists or they don't know how to track it down. Last year alone, over $22 billion was taken into custody by trustees, of which less than $1 billion was claimed.

Back to the business at hand. We have done the grunt work for you and are providing you with the sources we have. I know. Pretty cool. There are a lot of ways to find "lost" money that you may have never even thought about.

And we are just getting started. But it never ends. Another source of free money was just handed to me!

Fees

You know why so many people wear I LOVE NEW YORK shirts? Because New York attorney general Andrew Cuomo isn't afraid to stick it to people who deserve it. As of press time, he is putting the pressure on the big shot credit card companies JP Morgan and Chase to stop with the new $10 monthly fee.

Yes, another new fee.

This new fee went into effect in January 2009 and in late March, JP Morgan said they would stop the penalty and refund what has been collected so far. Any wild guess what they have collected in this short period of time?

84,000 cardholders. $4.4 million in refunds.

Holy smokes! $4 million in three months?!

The credit card company did what credit card companies are doing now. Making up new fees. They had the policy of allowing balance transfers for a one-time fee of ten bucks. Then wham bam outta the blue, they made this one-time fee an every month fee.

It's like hiring a hit man to go around and steal ten bucks from everybody. And steal it once a month.

Folks complained and the New York attorney general got involved. And now the big bad wolf of a credit card company is giving the money back!

Folks complained and the New York attorney general got involved.

They are giving back the rip-off fees! Are you a JP Morgan or Chase card holder? Be on the lookout for your share of the $4 million getting refunded! Receiving back money that has been taken from you is a sweet source of found money.

But I digress …

As you may have heard me mention in the past, the IRS is not exactly my favorite agency. But then again, who really adores the IRS?

Did you know that another source of found money is unclaimed tax refunds?

Read on!

CHAPTER 5

Tax Refunds

The Internal Revenue Service and I have been on close terms for some time. They like to scrutinize my every move. That is the price I pay for being who I am. No, I am not expecting any violin music to start. I am simply saying that being in my position and doing what I do, I get a little "extra attention" from time to time. I accept that.

Now let me give a little extra attention to the IRS and what they may have in store for you. How does $1.3 billion grab you?

The Taxman

I always feel the need to repeat myself when I say large numbers like that. $1.3 million is a lot, but $1.3 BILLION is staggering. What is going on with the $1.3 billion? That is the amount of unclaimed tax refunds from tax year 2005 alone.

Yep. Hundreds of thousands of taxpayers, for whatever reason, sometimes because the check was not delivered by the post office, did not receive their rightful refund. And those refunds add up.

The thing with IRS refunds is that there is a time deadline. And although I write this before the current April 15 deadline expires, the printing process and distribution process means that this little tidbit of info will just miss the cut. But the point is eternal and ever important no matter what day it is.

The $1.3 billion from tax year 2005 has to be claimed by April 15, 2009. There is a three year statute of limitations on tax returns. That means the 2005 return was due April 15, 2006, and the three year period expires April 15, 2009.

The statute works both ways. After April 15, 2009, the IRS dudes cannot audit your 2005 return. The statute has expired. It also means that after April 15, 2009, you cannot claim your 2005 refund. It goes back to the vault and becomes property of the US Treasury.

That part does not seem right to me.

Statutes

It may be too late for 2005 dollars, but the lesson here serves as a word of caution. If you are expecting a tax refund from here on out, do not let it slip through the cracks. The best way to avoid a lost check is to have the IRS deposit your refund directly into your bank account. This is quicker, too, and your money is there for you sooner than waiting for a check to come via the mailman.

If you opted for either direct deposit or mail delivery, pay attention to when you should receive your money. If it doesn't show up when expected, contact the Internal Revenue Service folks! The IRS even has a web page called "Where's my Refund?" simply because so many people inquire about the status of their refunds — probably because there are so many screw ups.

To research the missing refund, you need to know your social security number, your filing status (married filing jointly, single, married filing separately, head of household, or qualifying widow/

er), and the dollar amount of the refund you are expecting. ALWAYS keep a copy of the return you filed!

Find Your Refund

You simply go online to www.irs.gov, click on "Where's my refund?" and enter those three things, and hit Submit. The civil servants whose salaries we pay will look into your situation and see what happened to your money. Many times it is because they cannot deliver your check. The IRS does not allow mail to be forwarded. If this is the problem with your account, you can go online to update your current address.

And while I am on the topic, I need to give you a heads up. The IRS does not have emails that they send out to you. If you get an email claiming to be from the Internal Revenue Service, asking for your social security number, it is bogus. Mark it as spam. Never give your social security number in an email. Only enter it when you are on the IRS website.

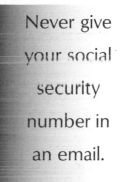

Never give your social security number in an email.

If you ever have a question about tax matters, you can call the toll-free customer service line at 800-829-1040. It has been my experience that they may, or may not, be able to help you. Hey, I call 'em as I see 'em. There is a refund line as well, 800-829-1954. Again, have your social security number, filing status, and refund amount ready.

Okay, back to the business at hand. Do you have a tax refund sitting out there due you? The odds are that some of you holding this book will. The numbers are huge. $1.2 billion went unclaimed for 2004 returns. $1.3 billion for the 2005 tax year. That equates to over a million people going without their refund.

Breaking it down by year, in one year (I think 2004, but it doesn't matter; it's the point here that matters), there were over 115,000 refund checks that were called undeliverable. Those checks totaled about $110 million. Yikes. $110 million and 115,000 bodies that the IRS says they could not locate. That is roughly $950 per person. Are you that person?

Blame it on the Mailman?

Every year, it is the same story. Millions of dollars do not get delivered. And there are checks that do get delivered, but never cashed. Huh?! My researchers tell me that $500,000,000 in refund checks goes uncashed. Every year! That fries my brain.

Believe me, when I get a check, it goes right to the bank. A diamond may be forever, but a check is not. You gotta cash it or deposit it right away, usually within sixty or ninety days. I don't think the three-year statute applies to checks.

I may not agree with the policy, but IRS refund checks are in the "use it or lose it" category. I hate to see you lose it.

If you have a check coming, make sure you get it. If you get a check, make sure you cash it.

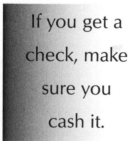

If you get a check, make sure you cash it.

Maybe you have a refund coming, but did not file a return. That is another way the Treasury coffers grow. They owe you money but you did nothing to claim it. Don't let that happen!

You can file a tax return late and not pay any penalty if you have a refund coming. There can only be a penalty on tax owed. No tax due, no penalty. Be warned that if you file a 2006 return that has a refund coming, and you have not filed 2007 and 2008 returns, they can withhold the refund until you file all outstanding years.

Often it happens that a person worked a job, had some tax withheld, would have been due a refund, but did not file a return. That tax withheld belongs to you. Again, I go back to the fact that if it is rightfully yours, don't you want it?

File the tax return and get it.

Do Not Be Intimidated

Some people are intimidated by the idea of taxes. Filing a return may not be as complicated as you think. Have a friend help you if you feel unsure of yourself or take advantage of the free tax help at the local IRS office or from community service volunteers. There are free programs at many public libraries and community centers across the country to help you file your return.

Besides missing checks and tax withheld that you should get but did not, there are other ways that the IRS could owe you money and you are not collecting it. Curious?

Ever heard of tax credits? Turn the page and read on.

CHAPTER 6

Tax Credits

If ever there was money that could be called FREE money, tax credits are it! There is nothing more gladdening to my old achy-breaky heart than money for nothing, and especially so when it comes from the cranky old IRS!

The world of the Internal Revenue Service and income taxes does not have to be as scary as people want to make it. File your return and you could be pleasantly surprised at the amount of money coming back to you.

Tax Credits = Free Money

Even if you had no tax withheld, there are tax credits that you could be entitled to. You need to file in order to claim them. Worth learning about, don't you think?

The tax world is bursting with tax credits. The most common that apply to many people are:

✔ First time homebuyer tax credit
✔ Child tax credit
✔ Earned income tax credit
✔ Credit for child and dependent care
✔ Education credit
✔ Saver's credit

Before I get too carried away, you can get the lowdown on tax credits at www.irs.gov or google the credit name. The IRS 800 number is also available for questions.

First Time Homebuyers Tax Credit

This credit is new and is a result of our tumultuous economy. Because it is new, many people are not aware of it or how it works. It is confusing because if you buy a house in 2009, you can claim this credit on your 2008 tax return or your 2009 return.

> If you buy a house in 2009, you can claim this credit on your 2008 tax return or your 2009 return.

If you are a first time homebuyer, 2009 looks to be a good year. Home prices are historically low and foreclosure bargains are everywhere. This new $8,000 credit applies to a home purchased in 2009 (before December 1, 2009), so if you are thinking about buying, it could be an added incentive.

Eight grand is not chump change. Even if you have already filed your 2008 return, there are ways to still claim this credit this year. I say get your money back as soon as possible. If you are a first time homebuyer, and there should be a lot of you this year, listen up.

From the Treasury website: "Under the American Recovery and Reinvestment Act of 2009, qualifying taxpayers who purchase a home before December 1 receive up to $8,000, or $4,000 for married individuals filing separately. People can claim the credit either on their 2008 tax returns due April 15 or on their 2009 tax returns next year." [Source: www.irs.gov/newsroom/article/0,,id=205416,00.html]

The credit is up to $8,000 ($4,000 if you are married filing separately). You are allowed to deduct ten percent of the purchase price of the home up to that $8,000 limit. If you buy a $900,000 home, ten percent would be $9,000, so you would be limited to the maximum of $8,000. If you buy a home for $500,000, you are allowed a credit of $5,000.

Maybe I should remind you that a tax credit is not a deduction. It completely wipes out tax. If you owed $8,000 in taxes but were eligible for the max $8,000 credit, you would owe ZERO — a big fat 0 — in tax.

I love tax credits!

This one is a little confusing because you can take it in 2008 even though the home purchase happens in 2009. The filing options per www.irs.gov are:

- ✔ **File an extension.** Taxpayers who haven't yet filed their 2008 returns but are buying a home soon can request a six-month extension to October 15. This step would be faster than waiting until next year to claim it on the 2009 tax return. Even with an extension, taxpayers could still file electronically, receiving their refund in as few as 10 days with direct deposit.

- ✔ **File now, amend later.** Taxpayers due a sizable refund for their 2008 tax return, but who also are considering buying a house in the next few months, can file their return now and claim the credit later. Taxpayers would file their 2008 tax forms as usual, then follow up with an amended return later this year to claim the homebuyer credit.

- ✔ **Amend the 2008 tax return.** Taxpayers buying a home in the near future who have already filed their 2008 tax return can consider filing an amended tax return. The amended tax return will allow them to claim the homebuyer credit on the 2008 return without waiting until next year to claim it on the 2009 return.

✔ **Claim the credit in 2009 rather than 2008.** For some taxpayers, it may make more financial sense to wait and claim the homebuyer credit next year when they file the 2009 tax return rather than claiming it now on the 2008 tax return. This could benefit taxpayers who might qualify for a higher credit on the 2009 tax return. This could include people who have less income in 2009 than 2008 because of factors such as a job loss or drop in investment income.

[Source: www.irs.gov/newsroom/article/0,,id=205416,00. html]

Be advised that you get less credit as your income goes up. If you are married filing jointly and make more than $150,000, you will not be able to take the full credit. If you are single and make more than $75,000, you will not be able to take the max credit either. Well, I am simplifying a bit when I say "if you make more than $xx." That figure is adjusted gross income, which is not the exact amount of your wages. If you are over the income limits and need help determining the maximum credit you are allowed, see the website, give the IRS a call, or ask your tax man.

This credit comes to us because of the American Recovery and Reinvestment Act, part of the new Obama administration. Visit www.Recovery.gov to learn more. This is what they — the people who wrote the act — have to say about it:

The American Recovery and Reinvestment Act is an unprecedented effort to jumpstart our economy, create or save millions of jobs, and put a down payment on addressing long-neglected challenges so our country can thrive in the 21st century. The Recovery and Reinvestment Act is an extraordinary response to a crisis unlike any since the Great Depression. With much at stake, the Act provides for unprecedented levels of transparency and accountability so that you will be able to know how, when, and where your tax dollars are being spent. Spearheaded by a new Recovery Board, this Act contains built-in measures to root out waste, inefficiency, and unnecessary spending. This website, Recovery.gov, will be the main vehicle to provide each and every citizen with the ability to monitor the progress of the recovery. [Source: www.Recovery.gov]

Lofty and wordy, yes, but an eight grand tax credit is a beautiful thing.

> An eight grand tax credit is a beautiful thing.

Child Tax Credit

I get a kick out of "IRS language." How does this sentence work for you: "You may be able to claim the child tax credit if you have a qualifying child"?

Hmm. You got kids? Let's see if they qualify as a "qualifying child."

1. Is a United States citizen or resident, or national;

2. Is under age 17 at the end of the calendar year;

3. Is your son, daughter, stepson, stepdaughter, legally adopted child, or a child placed with you for legal adoption, brother, sister, stepbrother, stepsister, foster child, or a descendant of any such person; AND

4. Shares with you the same principal residence for more than one-half of the tax year, or is treated as your qualifying child under the special rule for parents who are divorced, separated, or living apart.

You know what's funny? I tried to make those four qualifiers simpler to understand and they still sound a bit over the top. In # 4, I used the word "residence." The IRS used "place of abode."

Basically, for most of you, assuming you are a US citizen, if your child is still under age 17, you probably meet the requirements for "qualifying child." If you claim that kid as yours at the family picnic, you probably meet the requirements.

If your fifteen-year-old comes home pierced and tattooed and dyed her hair black and white, you may gasp, "That's not my kid." For purposes of the child tax credit, however, you will want to claim her.

What is the child tax credit? A little bonus in your pocket for those expensive offspring. Kids cost big bucks to clothe and feed. A little tax credit back your way is a good thing. If you want some in-depth reading on this credit, pick up Publication 672. If you have questions, as always, call the IRS or look up www.irs.gov.

In a nutshell, you get a credit of $1000 per little darling. If you have one child, your credit is $1000 (limited to income restrictions that will phase out the credit the more money you make. Married filing jointly, the income limit is $110,000; and single, it is $75,000).

If your tax due is $1,000, you apply the credit and dollar for dollar wipe out the tax. You owe nothing. If your tax bill was $1,400, you would only owe $400.

This credit is not refundable. That means if you owe $500 in tax and your credit is $1,000, you eliminate all tax, but do not get the extra $500 refunded to you.

Some credits are refundable. Even if you owe no tax, you still get the full credit money. Now that I really like!

To claim the credit, it is as easy as checking a box on the front of the return where you enter the names and social security numbers of your children.

Earned Income Tax Credit

The Earned Income Tax Credit (EITC) is a refundable credit. That means if you qualify for this credit, file your tax return! You get the money! This is one of the reasons the Treasury is bulging with unclaimed money. EITC folks are not filing to get their fair share.

The key words here are earned income. That means a job. If you have income that you earned from working, check into the requirements for this credit. And in case you were wondering, you do not have to have a child to qualify for this credit. You just have to have earned income.

The basic rules for this credit are:

✔ Must have a valid Social Security Number

✔ You must have earned income from employment or from self-employment.

✔ Your filing status cannot be married filing separately.

✔ You must be a U.S. citizen or resident alien all year, or a nonresident alien married to a U.S. citizen or resident alien and filing a joint return.

✔ You **cannot** be a qualifying child of another person.

✔ If you do not have a qualifying child, you must:

   o be age 25 but under 65 at the end of the year,

   o live in the United States for more than half the year, and

   o not qualify as a dependent of another person.

Okay. I think I've got that figured out. The next hurdle is income requirements.

For tax year 2008:

Earned income and adjusted gross income (AGI) must each be less than:

✔ $38,646 ($41,646 married filing jointly) with two or more qualifying children;

✔ $33,995 ($36,995 married filing jointly) with one qualifying child;

✔ $12,880 ($15,880 married filing jointly) with no qualifying children.

Tax year 2008 maximum credit:

✔ $4,824 with two or more qualifying children;

✔ $2,917 with one qualifying child;

✔ $438 with no qualifying children.

✔ And last but not least, investment income must be $2,950 or less.

Go to www.irs.gov to check the dollar amounts for each year, or if you have questions. Credits can be tricky to understand.

Sometimes the IRS gets a little long-winded in their explanations and I have succumbed to that, too.

Remember, if you have questions, call the toll-free IRS number or ask a friend or take advantage of the free local tax help. These credits are great money for you! Be sure to take advantage, if they apply to you!

> These credits are great money for you!

You can see that you do not have to have a child for this credit but if you do, you get more credit. Give that kid a hug. If you are married and file together and have two kids, you can get over $4,800 in free money. Holy cow! That could be a huge help to the household!

For tax year 2009 (due April 15, 2010), the money amounts are:

- ✔ $40,295 ($43,415 married filing jointly) with two or more qualifying children;

- ✔ $35,463 ($38,583 married filing jointly) with one qualifying child;

- ✔ $13,440 ($16,560 married filing jointly) with no qualifying children.

Tax year 2009 maximum credit:

- ✔ $5,028 with two or more qualifying children;

- ✔ $3,043 with one qualifying child;

- ✔ $457 with no qualifying children.

I cannot stress enough how many people are entitled to this EITC and do not claim it. If you want to read more, get IRS

Publication 596. If you qualify for EITC, you may also be entitled to a similar credit on your state tax return.

For the list of states that offer EITC (there are twenty-two as we go to print), check out www.irs.gov/individuals/article/0,,id=177866,00.html.

Before I move on to the next credit, there is one more thing you need to know about EITC. You can get a little advance credit in your paycheck throughout the year instead of waiting for the tax return. Yep! It is called Advance Earned Income Tax Credit.

> You can get a little advance credit in your paycheck...

There is a form you fill out and give to your employer, if you expect to qualify and have at least one child. A little extra in the paycheck is a nice option, if you want to take advantage of it. When you file your tax return at the end of the year, report the amount of the credit you have already received (it will be on your W-2 earnings statement from your employer) and file for the rest of the credit due you.

Visit www.irs.gov/individuals/article/0,,id=96466,00.html for all the detailed info on the Earned Income Tax Credit.

Credit for Child and Dependent Care Expenses

Do you pay someone to care for your kids who are under age 13 so you can go to work? Do you pay someone to care for your spouse or your dependent who cannot care for himself/herself? You may be entitled to a credit of 20% to 35% of those expenses.

For all the details, see Publication 503 or www.irs.gov. The same kind of rules for "qualifying" children apply.

In general, if you work and pay daycare, this credit is for you. You will have to identify the caregiver on the form and give the social security number, if you pay an individual, or tax ID number, if you use a daycare center.

Paying a babysitter while you go to Bunco night does not count here. Paying a babysitter while you work, or look for work, does count here. Follow the instructions for Form 2441 and it walks you through to easily compute the credit.

The credit varies from person to person because it is based on what you pay for child care and what your earned income is. For example, if you pay $3,000 for Little Junior's daycare and your income is over $43,000, you get 20% of the $3,000 as your credit, $600. And that is nothing to sneeze at.

If you pay $6,000 for two kids to go to daycare while you work, and have income less than $15,000, your credit is 35% of the $6,000. My math computes that to be a credit of $2,100. Nice found money!

The form shows the income limits and the percentage you are allowed. The total credit is limited to $5,000.

Education Tax Credits

Education tax credits can help offset the costs of higher education for you or your dependent. Schooling is not cheap and you need every break that comes your way. If you or your student is enrolled at least half time, check out these credits.

The Hope Credit applies for the first two years of college or vocational school. The credit can be up to $1,800 per student per year. If you have gone back to school and have a kid in college, you get double dips.

The second credit available is called the Lifetime Learning Credit. This credit applies to undergrad, graduate, and professional level degrees. It is not just the first two years like the Hope Credit.

This credit is 20% of the first $10,000 you pay in tuition and fees, up to a maximum of $2,000 per year.

You cannot claim the Hope Credit and the Lifetime Learning Credit for the same student in the same year. But if you have more than one student in your household, it is possible to claim both credits.

Watch the income limits. If you are married filing jointly and your income is over $116,000, you do not get these education credits. If your income is between $96,000 and $116,000, the amount of the credit is reduced.

To get the full scoop, check out www.irs.gov or get Publication 970. The form to claim these credits is Form 8863.

In case I have not mentioned it, all forms and publications are available for download at www.irs.gov.

Saver's Credit

The purpose of this credit is to help workers save for retirement and get a tax break now. If you put money into an IRA (Individual Retirement Account) or your employer's 401(k) plan, this Saver's Credit may apply to you.

The credit can be claimed by:

✔ Married couples filing jointly with incomes up to $53,000 in 2008 or $55,500 in 2009;

✔ Heads of Household with incomes up to $39,750 in 2008 or $41,625 in 2009; and

✔ Married individuals filing separately and singles with incomes up to $26,500 in 2008 or $27,750 in 2009.

Like other tax credits, the saver's credit can increase a taxpayer's refund or reduce the tax owed. Gotta love those tax credits. The maximum Saver's Credit is $1,000 for single filers and $2,000 for married couples.

A taxpayer's credit amount is based on filing status, adjusted gross income, tax liability, and amount contributed to qualifying retirement programs. Form 8880 is used to claim the saver's credit, and the instructions have details on how to figure the credit.

Per the IRS: For tax year 2006, the most recent year for which figures are available, saver's credits totaling almost $900 million were claimed on nearly 5.2 million individual income tax returns. Saver's credits claimed on these returns averaged $213 for joint filers, $149 for heads of household, and $128 for single filers.

Gotta love those tax credits.

What else you need to know to claim this credit:

✔ Eligible taxpayers must be at least 18 years of age.

✔ Anyone claimed as a dependent on someone else's return cannot take the credit.

✔ A student cannot take the credit. A person enrolled as a full-time student during any part of 5 calendar months during the year is considered a student.

Begun in 2002 as a temporary provision, the saver's credit was made a permanent part of the tax code in legislation enacted in 2006. To help preserve the value of the credit, income limits are now adjusted annually to keep pace with inflation. More information about the credit is on www.irs.gov. [www.irs.gov/newsroom/article/0,,id=200742,00.html]

> Tax credits are one way we can collect what is our due!

Maybe I have rattled on a bit long about tax credits, but think about it! All the ways that the government puts the screws to us, tax credits are one way we can collect what is our due! If you qualify for a tax credit, file your return and claim it! Unclaimed money goes back to the US Treasury. Shouldn't it go in your pocket instead?

Before I get off the topic of taxes, there is one more found money bonanza I need to tell you about. Did you know that you can deduct the sales tax you paid on the purchase of a new car?

Sales Tax Deduction for Vehicle Purchases

This is another new "recovery tool" that came to pass this year. The American Recovery and Reinvestment Act of 2009 allows you to take a deduction for the sales tax and any excise tax you paid on a new car, light truck, motorcycle, or motor home through 2009. Depending on the state and the purchase price, that can be a pretty hefty amount.

Even if you don't use Schedule A to itemize your deductions on your tax return, you still get to take this new deduction. Very nice.

There are limits of course. The deduction is limited to tax on $49,500 of the purchase price. If you bought a motor home that costs $50,000, you would have to prorate the tax. If your income is more than $125,000 (single) or $250,000 (married), the deduction is phased out. It gets wiped out completely for incomes exceeding $135,000 or $260,000.

If you made your new car purchase before February 17, 2009, you're screwed and don't get to take this credit. I don't know why they have to do it like that. Just make the deduction apply to the whole calendar year and keep it simple is my thought. But they didn't ask me.

Anyway, tell your friends, neighbors, and anyone you know who made a vehicle purchase to be sure to grab this special deduction.

And don't forget those tax credits!

CHAPTER 7

More Tax Talk

Some chapters could go on forever! But I like to break it into manageable pieces. There are tax credits galore. And they are among the best kept secrets of the government.

Some people accuse me of being dramatic when I talk about the government and how they don't want us to know much. I am not the only one who feels this way. *Smart Money* magazine ran an article in March 2009 titled, "10 Things the IRS Will Not Tell You."

The *Smart Money* folks share some great information that needs to see the light of day. (Source: www.smartmoney.com/personal-finance/taxes/10-things-the-irs-will-not-tell-you/?page=7)

Congress at Work

Remember how I discussed that Congress passes bills that are full of pork or earmarks? The big old $700 billion bailout bill was no different. The Congress added a little here and a little there. But did you hear about any of it?

The "green" eco-friendly Energy Policy Act of 2005 has been extended. Some more credits were added as well:

- ✔ Installing solar energy panels can net a credit of 30% of the cost involved

- ✔ www.solar-estimate.org can do just that — help estimate the cost

- ✔ Installing a wind energy system can net a credit of 30% of the cost involved. Up to $4,000.

- ✔ www.nrel.gov/eis/imby has more information on windmills

- ✔ $500 credit for installing energy efficient windows, central air system, or insulation.

I'll take that quick $500 please!

Uncle Sam

Another thing that Uncle Sam does not want you to know is that April 15 is not the drop dead date for filing your taxes. You can file for an extension and get an extension through October 15, with no fee or penalty. File 4868 by April 15 to get the extension.

If you get a refund, and over 112 million people do, there is no worry at all. If you will owe tax, you do have to pay that by the April 15 deadline. You can use last year's return as a ballpark estimate, if your situation has not changed much, and send in a check.

If you electronically file your tax return, you can expect your refund in about three weeks. Sometimes less. If you sent your return in through the mail, it usually takes six weeks to receive your refund.

If you don't get it, check on it. Every year, hundreds of thousands of checks — averaging nearly a grand per taxpayer — get thrown into the undeliverable pile through the post office. If you have moved, file a change of address form. If you have not received your check, follow up and ask taxpayer service when it was mailed or sent to your bank account.

Shhh...

The IRS won't tell you that sometimes they are wrong. When computing penalties, the feds have gotten their figures messed up. Always calculate it yourself to make sure you agree with their number. If not, call the IRS office or go to your local office and notify them that you have a different amount for what you owe.

The odds of getting audited are slim. Roughly 2% of all returns are assigned for audit. It does not matter what your income level is, all returns are subject to audit and you never know if yours will pop up. The IRS does not tell how they select returns, or what the hot issues are.

My advice is plain and simple. Keep receipts to back up your deductions. The auditors like to look at charitable deductions and business expenses, but anything on your tax return is fair game.

Many audits now are done through the mail. You will get a letter questioning an expense on your return, and you have to verify it.

An audit does not have to get you riled up. Many returns are sent in with too much tax paid! There is always the possibility that an audit can lead to a refund! The GAO — Government Accountability Office — reported that over 2 million people last year paid in too much!

Have someone check your return before you send it in. The average overpayment is nearly $500. That is money you need to keep!

If you get a letter from the IRS, a CP 2000 letter, stating that they have "corrected" your return and now you owe more, you can fight it. And you can get FREE help to do it. Contact your local taxpayer advocate — go to www.irs.gov/advocate to find. This person will provide advice and representation for FREE.

You want to know what else the IRS does not want you to know. They cannot protect your information any better than the credit card processing places do.

Identity theft and hackers can work their way into IRS systems, too. That seems outrageous, doesn't it? The large and powerful Oz, I mean Uncle Sam, can't promise to fend off cyber criminals and keep your social security number safe.

America is the most powerful nation on this planet and yet our government cannot guarantee us that our private financial information is tamper proof.

Free Tax Help

Another thing that is little known at tax time is that there is free help all around. The IRS has employees train volunteers to be tax preparers. All over communities, there are people who will help you.

One such place is a nonprofit organization called Ladder Up. This helpful coalition of volunteers was started in Chicago in 1994 by an accountant who still is the head of the agency. Ladder Up educates people on how to claim all the credits they are due and helps prepare their returns.

Normally, it costs about $150 to get a tax return prepared by a tax professional. Many folks just can't afford it. That is the first savings that Ladder Up provides, no charge for tax help. That's an extra $150 free money for the people they serve.

But it gets better. This group is now 16,000 volunteers strong and they have returned over $147 million to 84,000 families. Wow!

Ladder Up partners with local community agencies like the YMCA, churches, and schools. The volunteers who prepare the returns are trained to maximize the tax credits available to these folks. One gal discovered that she was owed $10,000 by the IRS!

That is a huge chunk of found money!

So when it comes to taxes, don't be intimidated. There are free help volunteers in many communities, and who knows, maybe you will find that the IRS is sending you a check for ten grand!

CHAPTER 8

Pensions

There is a huge jackpot of unclaimed pension benefits sitting there waiting to go to the rightful owners. Think about it. You, or your parents, worked long and hard for many years, and deserve that pension.

Companies come and go and change hands so many times now in our crazy world that pension plans can get terminated when a new owner takes over. The people due their money do not always get it. And people also change jobs and leave small pension amounts at that employer.

Don't Lose Your Pension

The Pension Benefit Guaranty Corporation (PBGC) reported that it is holding $133 million in unclaimed pension benefits. That figure was from 2007, so you can bet it is even more now.

The PBGC states that benefits range from a buck to over $600,000! The average per person payout is roughly $5,000.

The states with the most missing pension recipients and pension funds are New York, California, New Jersey, Texas, Florida, Pennsylvania, and Illinois. If you live in any of those states or worked in any of those states, you need to perk up. And no matter what state you live or work in, you need to make sure whether you do have unclaimed pension benefits out there that belong to you.

The PBGC has set up an online search directory similar to the ones we talked about earlier. Go to www.pbgc.gov/search. Search by your last name, company name, and the state where the company was headquartered.

Millions Unclaimed

Over the past few years, over 22,000 people have found $137 million in unclaimed pension benefits through this search tool! That is worth a minute of your time!

Regardless of how it happened, if you have benefits, you want them. Now. And to avoid getting lost in the future, make sure you tell your employer when you move or change names. And with the ever-changing structure of corporate America, you need to keep track of when your company moves or changes names. Any pension information that they send you should be filed so you know where to collect your benefits when the time comes.

> To avoid getting lost in the future, make sure you tell your employer when you move or change names.

If you are searching for pension benefits for a deceased family member, contact the PBGC at www.pbgc.gov. If you are a beneficiary, you may be able to collect the benefits. The folks at the Pension Benefits Guaranty Corporation will help you in that process.

Of course, you could try it the old-fashioned way and contact the employer directly. That can be a good first place to start, if you think you have some money in past pension plans. Contact the company or the plan administrator, if you know who that is.

I know one gal who changed jobs so often that she left a trail of small pensions, assuming that they would magically find her somewhere down the road. Maybe, maybe not. You need to be proactive and keep track of your assets.

Now that you know, keep up to date with your pension at your employer. Keep a record of the name of the plan, the dates that you worked there and, if you are really on the ball, write down the plan number and the employer identification number of your company. This information should be on a statement or on your paperwork when you enrolled in the pension plan.

I am all for finding lost money, and I am all for keeping track of the money we've got! If you want more info, the PBGC has a booklet called Finding a Lost Pension, available on the website. Check out www.pbgc.gov for pension resources.

CHAPTER 9

Life Insurance

The sad thing is that many life insurance policy benefits go unclaimed. It is hard enough to lose a loved one. That loved one had a life insurance policy for you, the family members. Your relative paid the premiums all those years and the benefits are not going to where he or she intended — you.

It is not wrong or greedy to pursue finding life insurance benefits. That money is sitting waiting to be collected by the beneficiaries.

It's Your Life

You are entitled to it, plain and simple.

Sometimes employers give life insurance policies. Sometimes banks will give small policies to their account holders. And of course, there are policies that a person buys through a major life insurance company.

When there is a death, the family members have to report it to the life insurance company in order to collect policy benefits, but if they do not know a policy exists, the company cannot issue the money.

Also in recent years, some of the major life insurance companies have changed the way they are structured. In something called demutualization they converted to stock ownership, which simply means that policyholders and their beneficiaries are entitled to receive stock and cash, plus the insurance benefits.

> In a single year, unclaimed life insurance benefits can be over $20 billion.

Companies like Met Life, Prudential, and John Hancock made this conversion. And when the switch occurred, the records were discovered to need updating.

John Hancock did not have accurate addresses for 400,000 policyholders.

Met Life had 60 million shares unclaimed.

Prudential had 1.2 million policyholders that they could not locate.

It happens all the time. People move and the forwarding order for the post office expires. People marry and divorce and change names. People die.

Get the picture? There many reasons why life insurance benefits get lumped into the unclaimed property pile.

Billions at Stake

In a single year, unclaimed life insurance benefits can be over $20 billion. The average claimed by heirs or owners of the policies is only about $1 billion. That means there are a lot of billions still unclaimed.

To find abandoned life insurance funds:

✔ Perform a search of the unclaimed property databases in each state that you or your loved one lived in

✔ Perform a search of the databases in each state that you or your loved one worked in

✔ Visit our friends at NAUPA, the National Association for Unclaimed Property Administrators — www.unclaimed.org

✔ Visit www.missingmoney.org

✔ Be a detective. What do I mean by that? If you are wondering about a deceased loved one's insurance benefits, you can be smart and track down some clues on your own

o Search bank books and checking accounts for payments made to life insurance companies.

o Search their records for anything at all that is insurance related.

o Contact the insurance agent who carried the house or car policies. They may also have life insurance policies on your family member.

o Contact the financial advisor. He or she may be aware of any life insurance policies.

o Contact the accountant or attorney of your loved one. They may be aware of policies and other items.

o Contact current and former employers.

o Look at the prior tax returns to see if there is any interest related to life insurance.

o Watch the mail in the year following the death. There may be premium notices or other mailings from insurance companies.

o Check state unclaimed property offices.

o If there is any possibility that life insurance may have been purchased in Canada, you can contact the Canadian Life and Health Insurance Association via phone 800-268-8099 or www.clhia.ca.

o Contact the National Association of Insurance Commissioners (NAIC) Life Insurance Company Location System. The main site is www.naic.org. The locator is https://external-apps.naic.org/orphanedpolicy/.

As you can see, the sky is the limit for ways to find these lost funds. If you learn of something we don't list here, please share the knowledge. We will be doing monthly Free Money newsletters to keep everyone up to date on all the options out there. I hope you subscribe to the newsletter!

It is worth the search time when you uncover assets.

Remember, when searching for lost funds, be it life insurance or bank accounts or whatever, keep in mind that money could be held in several states, not just the last address. If you — or your loved one — worked or lived anywhere, even for a short time, there may be money in those unclaimed offices. It is worth the search time when you uncover assets. Some states report the average disbursement is $1,000.

If you have $1,000 or several thousand out there for you, you will be glad that you took a few extra minutes to search all possible states.

My buddies are having a heyday with this search information. Some are finding little amounts and some are finding amounts that aren't so little! What are you finding?

CHAPTER 10

Veterans Benefits

Maybe your loved one was a veteran. Benefits may have been lost in the record keeping process of the Department of Veterans Affairs. Same story, people move, change names, or die.

For all the info on veterans' benefits, visit www.va.gov. The toll free telephone number for beneficiaries for veterans' pension benefits is 877-294-6380. The main line is 877-827-1000. For questions on life insurance, call 877-294-6380.

Get Your Due

The usual items that are found money for veterans' benefits are life insurance, burial allowances, and disability payments. Members of the armed forces, and their heirs, may be entitled to Adjusted Service Bonds (ASB) which were issued in registered form to World War I veterans, and Armed Forces Leave Bonds (AFLB), issued in registered form to World War II veterans as compensation for accumulated but unused leave.

If you have an issue with military pay that you believe was never received, that is handled by the Defense Finance and Accounting Service.

The personnel records are maintained in the National Personnel Records Center/Military Personnel Records office (NPRC-MPR). A form DD-214 is required to process most claims, including those for burial assistance, life insurance, and pensions. You can get this form via the internet at www.archives.gov.

Service members or beneficiaries who believe they may be entitled to unclaimed insurance should contact:

Office of Service Members Group Life Insurance (OSGLI)
290 West Mt. Pleasant Avenue
Livingston, New Jersey 07039
(800) 419-1473

To search the Veterans Unclaimed Insurance Funds database, which includes death awards, dividend checks, and premium refunds owed to missing current and former policyholders or beneficiaries arising from United States Government Life, National Service Life Insurance, Veterans Special Life Insurance, Veterans Reopened Insurance, and Service-Disabled Veterans Life programs (not SGLI or VGLI), go to: https://insurance.va.gov.

(Source: www.unclaimed.com/va_benefit.htm)

Veteran's Tax Credit

While I am on the topic of veterans, I want to share with you a free money tip, and in general, just a good thing to do. We need to honor our men and women who fight for our country and our freedom. There are many ways to do so. This is one way and it also gives you free money by way of a tax credit.

As I discussed earlier, tax credits are a beautiful thing.

I am not sure how many states utilize this kind of credit, but I have been alerted by a friend in Illinois that Illinois employers can earn an income tax credit of up to $600 annually for hiring Veterans of Operation Desert Storm, Operation Enduring Freedom, or Operation Iraqi Freedom.

Times are tough and many people need jobs. It makes sense to give a job to someone who served in the above-named military operations.

The tax credit is five percent of the total wages paid to every qualified veteran hired after January 1, 2008. If you have a business and have the ability to hire someone, hire a veteran and you can get an extra $600 as well as doing a good thing.

The rules as I know them: Veterans must work at least 185 days during the tax year for the employer to qualify for the Veteran's Tax Credit.

Visit www.veterans.illinois.gov and download Schedule 1299-D Income Tax Credits Form to file for this credit.

Let me know if your state has any kind of credit or free money for veterans or for hiring veterans. We will share the information in the upcoming Free Money newsletters.

CHAPTER 11

Social Security and Odds & Ends

I bet you are getting the idea now that the places that money is waiting for you are EVERYWHERE. All this lost money needs to be FOUND! Without spending a dime, you can be rolling in FREE MONEY!

Yet another area of unclaimed bucks is Social Security. Are you getting your due? Is your mama? Your grandmother? Your neighbor? Your best friend?

Every year about a half billion dollars in Social Security benefit checks are not cashed. Oh my word. The Social Security Administration sends out the checks and if they go uncashed or unclaimed, the government worker bees do nothing to find the folks.

So once again, the effort falls upon you.

Need Security?

You obviously need to know the social security number of anyone you want to search for benefits. You may be eligible for unclaimed benefits, if you are a beneficiary of a deceased loved one.

The Social Security Death Index (SSDI) has a record of reported deaths. This database maintains the social security number, date of birth, date of death, last known address, and payment of final benefit.

Contact the Social Security Administration office in your town or online at their website, www.ssa.gov.

To find a local office, go to https://secure.ssa.gov/apps6z/FOLO/fo001.jsp and enter your ZIP code.

So far, in ten chapters, we have covered a lot of ground. There is still much more to cover. Consider all the possibilities:

✔ Lost stock

✔ Unclaimed dividends

✔ Unclaimed inheritance

✔ IRAs and 401(k)s

✔ Swiss bank accounts
(I thought this was funny. Missingmoney.com has a link for dormant accounts here too — www.dormantaccounts.ch!)

Swiss Bank Accounts Anyone?

Maybe you have cash squirreled away in a Swiss bank account and forgot about it?! Maybe you have money buried in a box in the backyard. There are a gazillion kinds of found money — and I am not just talking about the change you find when you do the laundry, or under the couch cushions, or in your car.

Those small finds are great, but there is bigger bounty to be had. This information should get the wheels rolling in your head for more places to be proactive and search.

The odds are that there is cash with your name on it. In addition to all I have already expounded upon, the Securities and Exchange Commission (SEC) estimates there are three million lost stockholders who are entitled to unclaimed stock worth $10 BILLION!

And that's not all.

There's another $500 million of bond interest and stock dividends not cashed each year. Ch-ching! Companies merge and restructure all the time now. The constant change means a lot of information gets lost in the shuffle.

> The odds are that there is cash with your name on it.

Companies acquire and sell off companies nearly every day. It is hard to keep up. If you had stock in X company, you may now be eligible to receive shares of X company and Y company and Z company.

IRAs

There are also retirement accounts that have unclaimed money. About 50 million people have Individual Retirement Accounts (IRAs). At age 70 ½ you have to start taking withdrawals from the IRA. Some such withdrawals are unclaimed or considered abandoned.

Do you feel like the leprechaun looking for the pot of gold? This is not a mythical search for little green men or rainbows. This cash is real and available.

Many people also have retirement funds in their employer's plans — 401(k) plans. Every year about $850 million goes unclaimed. The usual reason for this missing money is that the company — the employer — has gone bankrupt or gone out of business. The money is left with the plan administrator and goes unclaimed by the rightful owners.

Who are the rightful owners? You!

Don't let another year go by without you getting what is rightfully yours.

Gift Cards

Another item that people seldom think about are gift cards. Yep. You get them as gifts and lose them or forget about them. Gift cards are big business, especially during the Christmas season. Don't know what to buy someone? Give them a gift card. We've all done it.

Over $70 billion is spent on gift cards and gift certificates. For whatever reason, many do not get redeemed. It is estimated that somewhere close to ten percent are never cashed in. That could be up to $7 billion.

Gift cards now are considered unclaimed property like all the other assets we have been discussing. Even though the actual gift card may have been lost, destroyed, or even expired, the value still exists and a refund may be entitled.

> Gift cards now are considered unclaimed property.

Gift cards are now part of the unclaimed asset search system. And what a search system it is. My buddy Paul found $273 owed to him by Bed, Bath & Beyond within seconds!

Love that NAUPA

The database at missingmoney.com maintained by the National Association of Unclaimed Property Administrators (NAUPA) is a veritable gold mine. There are more possibilities for free money than I have fingers and toes. And all I need are my fingers to do the search. What are you waiting for?

Start panning for your gold!

CHAPTER 12

Canada

I realize we have some readers from Canada or who may have unclaimed assets there. Canada operates a little different from the United States. First of all, Canadian banks have a legal obligation to attempt written notification of account owners after the second and fifth year of inactivity.

I like that. Not sure why the two and five, but a legal obligation to contact owners of the assets is a good thing.

In the ninth year of inactivity — year ten is when assets get transferred over to Bank of Canada — the Office of the Superintendent of Financial Institutions (OSFI) prepares a list of all unclaimed balances of $10 or more and the name of the owner. This list is published in the *Canada Gazette*, available at all public libraries.

O Canada

So Canada has a notice system in place. Very good.

Bank of Canada then becomes custodian when there has been no account activity for a ten year period and the owner cannot be contacted. Accounts worth $500 or more are held indefinitely until claimed. AND get this — interest is paid at the rate of 1.5% per year for a ten-year period.

Balances under $500 are retained for twenty years — ten years from the date of the last owner transaction at the bank, with an additional ten year custody period at Bank of Canada. To get the funds, a written claim must be received no later than December 31 of the account's "last year" — twenty years after the year of the last transaction.

> Revenue Canada... holding an estimated $8 million in unclaimed tax refunds since 1990.

Make sense so far? If more than $500, it sits forever. If less than $500, you have twenty years to claim it.

Canada has millions of unclaimed money. More than two-thirds of it is sums that are less than $500.

The Bank of Canada has a database to search as well. To check it out and do a search, visit ucbswww.bank-banque-canada.ca. You can also contact it the old fashioned way:

Dormant Account Section: Unclaimed Balances Services
Bank of Canada
234 Wellington
Ottawa, ON, K1A 0G9
(888) 891-6398

For tax refunds, their version of the IRS is called Revenue Canada. They are holding an estimated $8 million in unclaimed tax refunds since 1990. There is no time limit on claims, but no interest is paid on amounts refunded. Privacy legislation prevents publication of owner names. Citizens should contact their local tax office for additional information.

Unclaimed asset practices with regard to items other than bank accounts and tax refunds vary by province.

If you are looking into assets for a deceased loved one, you must be able to prove a blood relation. Have date of death and other information available. For info on "how to prove you are an heir," see http://www.attorneygeneral.jus.gov.on.ca/english/.

In British Columbia, the Ministry of Finance and Corporate Relations administers the Unclaimed Property Office and maintains a searchable database. This database serves this province only. See http://www.bcunclaimedproperty.bc.ca.

(Source: www.unclaimedassets.com/canada.htm)

CHAPTER 13

United Kingdom

And for our friends across the pond, unclaimed property is very much the case there as well.

An old report from London's *Financial Times* stated, "There is a sea of unclaimed assets sloshing around the financial system." Back in 1999, the low estimate of unclaimed funds was £77 billion.

You know that number has got to be more now.

The funds are the same kind of thing that happens here in the States. Old bank accounts, unclaimed pensions, life insurance policies, securities, dividends, unredeemed national savings certificates and premium bonds.

One item I found interesting was that the United Kingdom unclaimed asset pool contains winnings from their national lottery. Wow. People win the lottery and don't claim it. See what I mean that money is in unexpected places.

[Source: www.unclaimedassets.com/UK.htm]

CHAPTER 14

Free Medical Help

I think we have pretty well established that there are many opportunities out there for found money. Take it from someone else besides me:

> *"The chance that you or someone you know has*
> *unclaimed property is greater than you think.*
> *Finding out is free and easy."*
> —Alexi Giannoulias, Illinois State Treasurer

I think it is very exciting to have at our fingertips all the sources and resources to find money!

Another way of getting free money is not having to give up your own money and getting free services in return.

With the rising cost of living and shrinking incomes, many people need ways to cut back in the household budget and literally find some extra money. Well, here you go.

Medical-Mental Health

More than ever people are struggling with depression and other issues that can lead to more serious health problems. If you can get help early on, the better off you — and your family — will be.

There is a website called freementalhealth.com. And it offers exactly what it says. Many times people put off going to the doctor because money is tight and they think they should spend it on other things. And when it comes to emotional or mental health issues, we sometimes think we can handle it on our own.

Now you know that free help is out there. Take advantage of it. Use this website to find what you need.

If drugs or alcohol are a problem, there are free programs in many communities. You can use a local directory or use freementalhealth.com to find 24,000 locations for free clinics and drug rehab programs.

The site is free and confidential.

According to the site, "this site was set up so that you can type in anywhere in the US to find out what free drug or mental health treatment is available for free. Drugs, depression, anxiety, bipolar, schizophrenia. Also free help for children with autism, depression, anxiety, ADD or ADHD."

[Source: freementalhealth.com]

Prescriptions

Another huge expense is prescription medications. That alone can eat up the budget of a single elderly person on a fixed income.

Prescription help is available, too. Five million folks have discovered something called Partnership for Prescription Assistance. Visit www.pparx.org for the whole scoop.

In general, this service is a partnership of doctors, drug companies, health care providers, and patient advocate groups. Amen to that. The Partnership for Prescription Assistance helps patients who do not have prescription benefits through insurance to get the medicines they need, either through a public or private program.

Many people are now able to get their meds for free or just about free. This partnership is one stop shopping, giving access to 475 patient assistance programs and 180 programs offered through the drug companies.

> Many people are now able to get their meds for free or just about free.

Some people are not comfortable using the Internet, so the PPA has a toll free telephone number as well: 888-477-2669.

To get qualified you simply have to answer a few short questions. The site or the folks at PPA will guide you to a program. Forms for the programs are available for download or on the phone. If you need help filling out the form, someone from PPA will assist you.

The site has a link to Medicare prescription drug coverage as well.

If ever there was a need for free money, this area is it. Many people are hurting financially because of medical expenses. Prescriptions can be so expensive. Millions of people need this kind of assistance. Free money for meds!

Money for Meds

The Partnership for Prescription Assistance helps qualifying patients get the drugs they need. The system has access to more than 2,500 medicines. The PPA helps match patients to prescription programs that provide free or nearly free medicines.

There are no fees to use PPA and almost all of the programs offer their services free of charge. There are other imitator programs out there that try to rip you off. Don't fall for it. This Partnership will not charge you.

[Source: www.pparx.org]

> Many states offer discounted drug programs.

Besides Partnership, there are many other prescription drug programs. If you don't have health insurance, or if your insurance doesn't include good prescription drug benefits, look for generic drug offers at many major supermarkets and drug stores. Many stores offer great deals now.

Also, many states offer discounted drug programs. Look for your state at covertheuninsured.org/content/resources-uninsured (see Table 2).

You can also check these private groups that offer prescription assistance:

HealthWell Foundation — www.healthwellfoundation. org/index.aspx

FamilyWize discount drug card — www.familywize.com/ index.aspx

Needy Meds — www.needymeds.org

Rx Assist — www.rxassist.org/docs/medicare-and-paps.cfm

Rx Hope — https://www.rxhope.com

Chronic Disease Fund — www.cdfund.org/Patient/ patient1.aspx

The Access Project — www.atdn.org/access/pa2.html

[Source: www.cnn.com/2009/HEALTH/02/12/ep.health.insurance.help/index.html?iref=mpstoryview]

Some states have drug assistance programs. Google "prescription programs" and the name of your state. For example, New York has a state program: applications are available at pharmacies and community organizations, online at nyprescriptionsaver.fhsc.com or by a toll-free number: 800-788-6917. Workers are eligible, if they're 50 to 64 years old and making up to $35,000 a year, or married with household income of $50,000.

Odds are your state has a prescription program.

There are also co-pay programs that offer financial assistance for some health care costs. If you have medical issues, you can try these organizations.

Program:	**American Kidney Fund**
Mission:	With help from AKF, dialysis patients are able to maintain their health insurance coverage. AKF also provides assistance with expenses that insurance will not cover, such as transportation to dialysis, medications, special diet, kidney donor expenses, and other treatment essentials. AKF's specialty programs help patients afford treatment during emergency travel and recover from natural disasters.
URL:	www.kidneyfund.org
Email:	patientservice@kidneyfund.org
Address:	6110 Executive Blvd., Suite 1010 Rockville, MD 20852
Phone:	800-638-8299
Assistance:	National Medicare Prescription Drug Assistance Insurance Premium Assistance Other Patient Support

Program:	**Association of Community Cancer Centers**
Mission:	ACCC is the national multidisciplinary organization that focuses on enhancing, promoting, and protecting the entire continuum of quality cancer care for patients.
URL:	www.accc-cancer.org
Address:	11600 Nebel Street, Suite 21, Rockville, Maryland, 20852-2557
Phone:	301-984-9496
Fax:	301-770-1949
Assistance:	National Prescription Assistance

Program:	**CancerCare**
Mission:	CancerCare is a national nonprofit organization that provides free, professional support services to anyone affected by cancer: people with cancer, caregivers, children, loved ones, and the bereaved. CancerCare programs, including counseling, education, financial assistance, and practical help are provided by trained oncology social workers and are completely free of charge.
URL:	www.cancercare.org
Email:	info@cancercare.org
Address:	275 Seventh Ave., Floor 22, New York, NY 10001
Phone:	800-813-4673
Fax:	212-712-8495
Assistance:	National Prescription Assistance
	Other Patient Support

Program:	**Candlelighters Childhood Cancer Foundation**
Mission:	Our mission is to provide information and awareness for children and adolescents with cancer and their families, to advocate for their needs, and to support research so every child survives and leads a long and healthy life.
URL:	www.candlelighters.org
Email:	staff@candlelighters.org
Address:	P.O. Box 498, Kensington, MD 20895-0498
Phone:	800-366-2223 or 301-962-3520

Program:	**Caring Voice Coalition, Inc.**
Mission:	Comprehensive help for the needs of patients with serious, chronic illnesses
URL:	www.caringvoice.org
Email:	CVCInfo@caringvoice.org
Address:	Caring Voice Coalition, Inc., 8249 Meadowbridge Road, Mechanicsville, VA 23116
Phone:	888-267-1440
Assistance:	National Medicare Prescription Drug Assistance
	Insurance Copayment Assistance
	Insurance Premium Assistance
	Insurance Counseling and Advocacy
	Other Patient Support

Program:	**Chai Lifeline**
Mission:	Chai Lifeline is a not for profit organization dedicated to helping children suffering from serious illness as well as their family members. They offer a comprehensive range of services to address the multiple needs of patients, parents, and siblings.
URL:	www.chailifeline.org
Email:	info@chailifeline.org
Address:	International Office, 151 West 30th Street, New York, NY 10001
Phone:	(877) CHAI LIFE
Fax:	212-465-0949
Assistance:	National Insurance Copayment Assistance
	Insurance Premium Assistance
	Other Patient Support

Program:	**Chemocare.com**
Mission:	This organization provides links to other resources for prescription assistance.
URL:	www.chemocare.com/lifeduring/financial_assistance_programs_for.asp

Program **Chronic Disease Fund, Inc. (CDF)**

Mission: CDF's focus is to provide assistance to those under-insured patients who are diagnosed with chronic or life altering diseases that require the use of expensive, specialty therapeutics.

URL: www.cdfund.org

Email: info@cdfund.org

Address: 10880 John W. Elliott Drive, Suite 400, Frisco, TX 75034

Phone: (877) YOUR-CDF

Assistance: National Prescription Assistance

Program: **Geriatric Services of America**

Mission: Help chronic respiratory disease patients by providing education, support, equipment, and life-saving medications quickly and directly to the patient's home.

URL: www.geriatricservices.com

Address: Geriatric Services of America, Inc., 5030 S. Mill Ave. D-23, Tempe, AZ 85282

Phone: 800-307-8048

Program: **HealthWell Foundation**

Mission: The HealthWell Foundation addresses the needs of individuals who cannot afford their insurance copayments, premiums, coinsurance, or other out-of-pocket health care costs.

URL: www.healthwellfoundation.org

Email: info@healthwellfoundation.org

Address: P.O. Box 4133, Gaithersburg, MD 20878

Phone: 800-675-8416

Fax: 800-282-7692

Assistance: National
Insurance Copayment Assistance
Insurance Premium Assistance
Prescription Assistance
Other Patient Support

Program: **Hunterdon County Medication Access Partnership (HCMAP)**

Mission: HCMAP connects concerned individuals, congregations, businesses, and government organizations to increase awareness and access to affordable prescription medication for Hunterdon County residents in need.

Email: mark.peters@bms.com

Address: 23 Timberwick Drive, Flemington, NJ 08822

Phone: 609-897-2866

Assistance: Prescription Assistance

Program: **International Oncology Network (ION)**

Mission: To keep affordable medications within patients' reach, many of ION's pharmaceutical partners offer Patient Assistance Programs to provide free or discounted medications to people who may not be able to afford their needed medications.

URL: https://www.iononline.com

Email: memberid@iononline.com

Address: International Oncology Network (ION), An AmerisourceBergen Specialty Group Company, 3101 Gaylord Parkway, Frisco, TX 75034

Phone: 888-536-7697 Ext: 6847

Fax: 888-329-3893

Assistance: National
Prescription Assistance

Program: **Leukemia and Lymphoma Society**

Mission: The Leukemia & Lymphoma Society is the world's largest voluntary health organization dedicated to funding blood cancer research, education and patient services. The Society's mission: Cure leukemia, lymphoma, Hodgkin's disease and myeloma, and improve the quality of life of patients and their families. Since its founding in 1949, the Society has invested more than $550.8 million for research specifically targeting blood cancers.

URL: www.leukemia.org
Phone: 800-955-4572
Assistance: National
               Insurance Copayment Assistance
               Insurance Premium Assistance
               List Organizations that Provide Insurance Counseling
               and Advocacy
               Lists Organizations that provide Prescription
               Assistance

Program: **MEDBANK of Maryland, Inc.**
Mission: MEDBANK is a non-profit organization dedicated
               to accessing free prescription drugs for low-income,
               chronically ill Marylanders.
URL: www.medbankmd.org
Email: rnmcewan@medbankmd.org
Address: P.O. Box 42678, Baltimore, MD 21284
Phone: 877-435-7755
Fax: 410-821-9265
Assistance: Prescription Assistance

Program: **National Children's Cancer Society**
Mission: The mission of The National Children's Cancer
               Society is to improve the quality of life for children
               with cancer and their families by providing financial
               and in-kind assistance, advocacy, support services,
               and education.
URL: www.beyondthecure.org
Email: survivorship@children-cancer.org
Address: One South Memorial Drive, Suite 800, St. Louis,
               MO 63102
Phone: (800) 5-FAMILY
Fax: 314-241-1996

Program:	**National Organization for Rare Disorders**
Mission:	The National Organization for Rare Disorders (NORD), a 501(c)3 organization, is a unique federation of voluntary health organizations dedicated to helping people with rare "orphan" diseases and assisting the organizations that serve them. NORD is committed to the identification, treatment, and cure of rare disorders through programs of education, advocacy, research, and service.
URL:	www.rarediseases.org
Email:	orphan@rarediseases.org
Address:	55 Kenosia Avenue, P.O. Box 1968, Danbury, CT 06813-1968
Phone:	203-744-0100
Fax:	203-798-2291
Assistance:	National
	Insurance Copayment Assistance
	Insurance Premium Assistance
	Prescription Assistance

Program:	**Needy Meds**
Mission:	NeedyMeds is a 501(3)(c) non-profit with the mission of helping people who cannot afford medicine or health care costs. The information at NeedyMeds is available anonymously and free of charge.
URL:	www.needymeds.com
Email:	info@needymeds.com
Address:	NeedyMeds, Inc, P.O. Box 219, Gloucester, MA 01931
Phone:	978-865-4115
Fax:	419-858-7221
Assistance:	National
	Medicare Prescription Drug Assistance
	Insurance Copayment Assistance
	Prescription Assistance

Program:	**Patient Access Network Foundation (PAN)**
Mission:	The Patient Access Network Foundation provides financial support for out-of-pocket costs associated with a wide range of drugs, to treat a number of conditions.
URL:	https://www.patientaccessnetwork.org
Email:	contact@patientaccessnetwork.org
Address:	P.O. Box 221858, Charlotte, NC 28222-1858
Phone:	1-866-316-PANF (7263)
Assistance:	National
	Prescription Assistance

Program:	**Patient Advocate Foundation Co-Pay Relief**
Mission:	Patient Advocate Foundation's Co-Pay Relief (CPR) Program provides direct co-payment assistance for pharmaceutical products to insured Americans who financially and medically qualify.
URL:	www.patientadvocate.org
Email:	help@patientadvocate.org
Address:	700 Thimble Shoals Blvd., Suite 200, Newport News, VA 23606
Phone:	800-532-5274
Fax:	757-873-8999
Assistance:	National
	Medicare Prescription Drug Assistance
	Prescription Assistance

Program:	**Patient Services Incorporated**
Mission:	Patient Services Incorporated (PSI) is a non-profit organization primarily dedicated to providing health insurance premium assistance, pharmacy co-payment assistance and co-payment waiver assistance for persons with specific expensive chronic illnesses.
URL:	www.uneedpsi.org
Email:	uneedpsi@uneedpsi.org
Address:	P.O. Box 1602, Midlothian, VA 23113
Phone:	800-366-7741

Fax: 804-744-5407
Assistance: National
                 Medicare Prescription Drug Assistance
                 Insurance Copayment Assistance
                 Insurance Premium Assistance
                 Insurance Counseling and Advocacy
                 Prescription Assistance

Program: **The Center for Medicare Advocacy**
Mission: The Center for Medicare Advocacy, Inc. is a national
                 non-profit, non-partisan organization that provides
                 education, advocacy, and legal assistance to help
                 elders and people with disabilities obtain Medicare
                 and necessary health care. The Center was established
                 in 1986. They focus on the needs of Medicare benefi-
                 ciaries, people with chronic conditions, and those in
                 need of long-term care. The organization is involved
                 in writing, education, and advocacy activities of
                 importance to Medicare beneficiaries nationwide. The
                 Center's central office is in Connecticut, with offices
                 in Washington, D.C., and throughout the country.
URL: www.medicareadvocacy.org
Address: P.O. Box 350, Willimantic, CT 06226
Phone: 860-456-7790
Assistance: Medicare Prescription Drug Assistance

As always, contact information changes, but this information was accurate to our knowledge when we went to print.

[Source: https://www.pparx.org/copay.php]

Medical

There are also private foundations that help with medical bills. For example, the Ray Tye Medical Aid Foundation states its mission as: "to facilitate access to medical treatments for financially vulnerable individuals in our society, thereby assuring equal access to specialized, life-saving medical evaluation, diagnosis, treatment and rehabilitation to all."

Everybody deserves decent health care. Everybody, no matter how much (or little) money you have. To request aid, click www.ray-tyemedicalaidfoundation.org/contact-us/medical-aid-request/.

> Everybody deserves decent health care.

This foundation also offers health assistance and hope around the world. In February 2009, a sixteen-year-old girl from Afghanistan was given a new life. She had broken her jaw at age eight, and it had welded together as it healed. She thus had a difficult time eating or speaking, and was in constant pain.

Thanks to a group called Healing the Children, she was brought to New York for miracle surgery. The Ray Tye Foundation paid for the surgery, giving her back a normal life. This medical aid foundation and others like it provide medical care for people here and all over the world.

Maybe you don't have a life shattering (or jaw shattering) incident, but need help with the medical bills. As I always advocate, negotiate!

Where there is a will, there is a way. If you don't have medical insurance, you may avoid going to the doctor because you feel you can't afford it. Sound like anyone you know?

There is a possibility for a little discount! That means found money for you to apply to other things!

Negotiate

Let me tell you a true story. And it's about a doctor. This doc, a plastic surgeon, was switching insurance companies and there was a window of time in between when he had no insurance coverage.

As Murphy's law would have it, he got hurt. He was playing baseball with his son and somehow fell on his elbow and hurt it badly. He was told he needed surgery immediately. And then he had to confess that he had no insurance.

It is odd for a doctor to not have insurance, but what he did, we all can do. He negotiated his costs!

It didn't matter that he was a doctor. He, as a patient, needed services just like everybody else. He did not want to pay the full cost of the surgery. He talked to the doctors at the immediate care clinic. He got his payment down from $4800 to $2400!

When you don't have insurance, there is no middle man. Talk to the doctor and the clinic. Explain that you can pay x amount. There is no insurance company to hassle with so odds are in your favor. If you are up front and frank and willing to negotiate, you may be surprised at the outcome.

This good doctor said it best: "You should always ask. Why wouldn't you try?"

I agree 100%.

The same article on CNN.com I referred to earlier also offers tips on getting found money for any doctor visits. There are places that help you find free care:

✔ Healthcare Advocacy — www.healthcareadvocacy.org

✔ Patient Advocate Foundation — www.copays.org

✔ Patient Services Incorporated — www.uneedpsi.org/
CMS400Min/index.aspx

Insurance

When it comes to insurance coverage, you don't have to go without just because you are in between jobs. You can still have your employer's insurance; the kicker is that if you go on COBRA insurance, you have to pay the premium instead of your old company.

Many times, it is cheaper to get insurance yourself. Check out this website to help you get the best deal: ehealthinsurance.com. Lots of great info there!

Maybe you are fit as a fiddle and go roll the dice and live without health insurance. You don't want to take the chance with your kids though. There is a program called SCHIP, State Children's Health Insurance Program, that offers discounted coverage.

The SCHIP website gives a state-by-state directory of programs. You can check it out at www.insurekidsnow.gov/states.asp or call 877-KIDS-NOW.

There are other government programs, too. Your entire family may qualify for insurance from a state high-risk pool, if you live in a state that has one. To find out about your state, check out www. naschip.org/states_pools.htm.

If you think you might qualify for Medicaid, see this state-by-state Medicaid directory at covertheuninsured.org/content/resources-uninsured.

Disease Help

If you have a specific disease, there are foundations that provide financial aid for your medical treatment. Some of these organizations include:

- ✔ Heart Disease: Heart Support of America
- ✔ Kidney Disease: American Kidney Fund
- ✔ HIV/AIDS: The Access Project
- ✔ Hepatitis: The Access Project
- ✔ Cancer: Cancer Care Assist
- ✔ Various Diseases: Caring Voice Coalition
- ✔ Other Rare Diseases: National Organization for Rare Diseases
- ✔ Vision Care: EyeCare America and Vision USA

Ever avoid going to the doctor because you didn't want to pay the bill? You are not alone. Find a place that you can afford. Find a place that's FREE.

There are federally funded health care centers all across the US. Even if you have no medical insurance, you pay what you can afford, based on your income. These health centers are located in cities and rural areas.

They will provide:

- ✔ checkups when you're well
- ✔ treatment when you're sick
- ✔ complete care when you're pregnant
- ✔ immunizations and checkups for your children
- ✔ dental care and prescription drugs for your family
- ✔ mental health and substance abuse care if you need it

To find a free clinic near you, type in your address at Find a Health Center, www.findahealthcenter.hrsa.gov.

Many people are out of work these days and that means people are going without insurance. It doesn't have to be so. Did you know that many part-time employers give benefits? Yep, you can get health insurance even if you don't work full time. Here is a sample of who pays part-timers benefits:

- ✔ Target
- ✔ Starbucks
- ✔ Lowe's
- ✔ IKEA
- ✔ Trader Joe's
- ✔ Whole Foods
- ✔ Barnes & Noble
- ✔ Nordstrom
- ✔ Land's End
- ✔ Nike
- ✔ JCPenney

Dental

Another aspect of health care is dental expenses. Going to the dentist can be expensive, so some people put it off and then a small problem becomes a major toothache!

Taking a peek at the www.medicare.gov, you will learn that there are programs that help out millions of folks. State Medicaid programs assist with medical and dental expenses and eyeglasses.

The National Foundation of Dentistry for the Handicapped (NFDH) provides services to the elderly, the disabled, and others.

There is a network of thousands of dentists who donate their time and even make house calls. For more information on this network and their service, visit www.nfdh.org. You can link directly to your state to find donated services in your community.

Dental schools are another great source of free services or highly discounted dental care. If you have a dental college in your community or a neighboring one, it could be worth your while to check it out and make the drive. Dental expenses, if paid at full, cost can be outrageous. Why pay full price if you don't have to? To find a dental college, contact: www.adea.org.

Eyeglasses

Sometimes people put off eye exams and new glasses because of the expense, too. Pearle Vision and LensCrafters both offer discounts to seniors and other groups. If you are a senior, you get LOTS of free money discounts through AARP, the Association of American Retired Persons. Take advantage. Go to www.AARP.com.

AAA members get discounts on eyeglasses, too. For kids too! Check out your AAA membership or look it up online. You can also go online to Pearle Vision or LensCrafters (www.pearlevision.com and www.lenscrafters.com) or go to the store location in your town. And if you have a Sear's store with an eyeglass store, they offer discounts too through AAA! (See www.searsoptical.com.)

Cheap glasses and cheap contacts and cheap eye exams. Free money for you.

Free Glasses

Target stores that have an optical department offer FREE eyeglasses for kids age 12 and under. These special promotions are not always in effect, but at press time, Target was promoting their optical service.

Pay attention to your local stores and community organizations. Different opportunities await at different times of the year. Ask. In person, online, or over the phone. Talk to friends, coworkers, family. They can be a good source for freebies.

You need to be a resource to people you know as well. Tell them that Target has offered free eyeglasses for kids. A current prescription from the eye doctor is all that is needed. There are many frames to choose from and there is no cost at all. Even more beautiful is that there are no income limits placed on this program. No adults are allowed, but kids age twelve and under are eligible.

What a great deal. Kids break their glasses and can get new ones. Kids who need a prescription change can get glasses. Kids who can't see the board and struggle in school can see the whole world in a whole new way by getting glasses.

> Target has offered free eyeglasses for kids.

To make sure this deal is still going on, check www.target.com or call your local Target store.

If you or your child are in need of eyeglasses, check with your state for state assistance. Many states have programs that provide free eye exams and/or glasses. Check with your county as well. Maybe your health care clinic has a program or can steer you to one.

There is a program in New York City that provides eyeglasses to school children. The Kress Vision Program has been doing so since the year 2000. This nonprofit organization works with the University Downtown Hospital to provide vision services for free to residents of New York. Visit www.downtownhospital.org/pages/3034/index.htm for more information on this program.

I doubt these types of programs offer designer frames for free, but the selection is good and the price is right — FREE!

Don't forget that most local Lion's Clubs (www.lionsclubs.org) provide free eyeglasses to their local communities. If you need an exam, try Vision USA. You apply and after they process your request, you receive a form that you take to a local eye doctor for a free eye exam for you or your child.

A volunteer organization called Prevent Blindness works with state, local, and national governments to provide eye screenings and eye care. They have several networks within local communities. For further details, visit www.preventblindness.org, www.diabetes-sight.org, or contact the PBA Vision Health Resource Center (1-800-331-2020).

As you can see (pun intended), there are many places out there willing and waiting to assist you with glasses and/or eye exams. There is another organization who claims, "we help when no one else can." For eyeglasses and eye exams, you can contact New Eyes for the Needy. To apply, you can contact a social service agency in your area, the school nurse at your child's school, or contact the organization directly at www.neweyesfortheneedy.org or send in your application form and prescription to:

New Eyes for the Needy
P.O. Box 332
Short Hills, NJ 07078

I hope this makes you realize that there are a gazillion ways to get what you want and you do not have to pay an arm and a leg for it. Use your creativity when thinking up resources and always ask that resource to refer you to the next one.

For example, you may have just received gorgeous new eyeglasses for you or your spouse or one of your kids. Or maybe you have been only getting information; you can always ask:

> One referral leads to the next and the next.

"Do you know of any other agencies, companies, or organizations that offer free eye exams?"

One referral leads to the next and the next. "Say, do you know of any agencies, companies or organizations that offer free dental work?" Or whatever it is that you may be looking for.

Aid is There

Okay, I think you get the idea.

And I think you can see how medical/dental/prescription help can be there for you now that you know where to look.

You also know that you can negotiate medical expenses. You can negotiate just about anything in this world! Every situation, always ask yourself if that is the best they can do and then ask them. When you show what you can pay and what you cannot, you will have people willing to work with you.

Especially in this economy, folks are even more willing. They want something as opposed to nothing.

If you get away with paying nothing, even better.

CHAPTER 15

Free Legal

I know many people who operate under the principle: never pay full price for anything. It makes sense. If you can get an item, be it a car or a pair of jeans, on sale, why in the world should you pay full price? You shouldn't. Paying retail is overpaying.

When you pay a reduced or discounted price, that is found money. More money in your pocket is the goal. And there are many ways to achieve that goal.

Free Legal Eagles

If you can get free or reduced medical care, dental care, or prescription medicines, why in the world should you pay full price? You don't need to pay "retail" for anything. Another little-known gold mine is free legal service.

Sometimes in life there comes a need for legal advice, and lawyers, as we all know, can be very expensive. You don't want to pay some guy by the minute when there are free options available to you.

The American Bar Association has a network of legal professionals who do pro bono work (that means you do not pay). You can search state by state to find legal help in your community.

✔ Visit www.abanet.org/legalservices/probono/directory.html and then click on your state.

✔ Another option is findlegalhelp.org. This site, too, has links to free legal help in your state.

✔ Go to www.abanet.org/legalservices/findlegalhelp/home.cfm for a quick search.

All states have tons and tons of free legal services. An amazing amount of legal aid is offered! All those lawyer jokes don't apply to the attorneys giving pro bono work. No matter where you live, you can click and pick from a wealth of agencies.

For example, if you live in California, with one click and in a matter of seconds, you can look into all of the following:

Greater Bakersfield Legal Assistance Inc.
615 California Avenue
Bakersfield, CA 93304
(805) 325-5943
www.gbla.org

Central California Legal Services
1401 Fulton Street, Suite 700
Fresno, CA 93721
(559) 441-1611
www.centralcallegal.org

Neighborhood Legal Services of Los Angeles County
1102 E. Chevy Chase Drive
Glendale, CA 91205
(818) 896-5211
www.nls-la.org

Inland Counties Legal Services Inc.
1040 Iowa Avenue, Suite 109
Riverside, CA 92507
(909) 368-2555
www.inlandlegal.org

Legal Services of Northern California Inc.
517 12th Street
Sacramento, CA 95814
(916) 551-2150
www.lsnc.net

Legal Aid Society of Orange County Inc.
2101 N. Tustin Ave.
Santa Ana, CA 92705
(800) 834-5001
www.legal-aid.com

California Indian Legal Services Inc.
609 S. Escondido Blvd.
Escondido, CA 92025
(760) 746-8941
www.calindian.org

Bay Area Legal Aid
405 14th Street, 9th Floor
Oakland, CA
(510) 663-4744
www.baylegal.org

Legal Aid Foundation of Los Angeles
1102 South Crenshaw Boulevard
Los Angeles, CA 90019-3111
(800) 399-4529
www.lafla.org

Legal Aid Society of San Diego Inc.
110 South Euclid Avenue
San Diego, CA 92114
(619) 262-0896
www.lassd.org

California Rural Legal Assistance Inc.
631 Howard Street, Suite 300
San Francisco, CA 94105-3907
(415) 777-2752
www.crla.org

Also, for free legal aid referrals and information in California, you can visit www.lawhelpcalifornia.org. See what I mean by how much information is available? That is just for one state.

Another search method is to google "legal aid" followed by the name of your county in your state.

> Google "legal aid" followed by the name of your county in your state.

Just to show the wealth of information and legal service opportunities, I clicked on Pro Bono for California again from the same site, findlegalhelp. Here are the results (source: www.abanet.org/legalservices/findlegalhelp/pb.cfm?id=CA):

California Lawyers for the Arts
Primary Address: 1641 18th St .
City: Santa Monica
State: CA
Zip Code: 90404-3807
General Phone: 310 998-5590
Fax: 310-998-5594
Intake Phone: 310-998-5590
Counties Served: Statewide
Case Types: Bankruptcy, Consumer, Employment, Health, Housing, Immigration, Individual Rights, Real Estate, Torts, Wills
Other Case Types: Arts/Entertainment Issues
Case Restrictions: CLA serves artists and arts organizations as well as general individuals with arts related issues
Website: www.calawyersforthearts.org/legalservices.html

California Lawyers for the Arts
Primary Address: Bldg C Fort Mason Center
City: San Francisco
State: CA
Zip Code: 94123
General Phone: 415-775-7200
Fax: 415-775-1143

Intake Phone: 415-775-7200 x547
Counties Served: Statewide
Case Types: Bankruptcy, Dissolution of Marriage, Employment, Health, Housing, Immigration, Individual Rights, Public Benefits, Real Estate, Torts, Wills
Other Case Types: Intellectual Property, General Business
Website: www.calawyersforthearts.org/legalservices.html

Disability Rights Education and Defense Fund Inc.
Primary Address: 2212 6th St.
City: Berkeley
State: CA
Zip Code: 94710-2219
General Phone: 510-644-2555
Fax: 510-841-8645
Counties Served: Nationwide
Case Types: Education, Individual Rights
Other Case Types: Civil Rights, Disability
Website: www.dredf.org

San Francisco Lawyers Committee Emergency Political Asylum Program
Primary Address: 301 Mission St
City: San Francisco
State: CA
Zip Code: 94105
General Phone: 415-543-9444
Fax: 415-543-0296
Counties Served: San Francisco
Case Types: Immigration

Alameda County Bar Association Volunteer Legal Services Corporation
Primary Address: 610 Sixteenth Street 426
City: Oakland
State: CA
Zip Code: 94612
General Phone: 510-893-7160
Fax: 510-893-3119
Intake Phone: 510-893-7160
Counties Served: Alameda
Case Types: Adoption, Bankruptcy, Community Economic Development, Consumer, Child Custody, Dissolution of Marriage, Domestic Violence, Elder Law, Housing, Immigration, Public Benefits
Case Restrictions: LSC restrictions. 1) must be residents of Alameda County or have a case in Alameda County 2) income restrictions = 125% of the federal poverty level.
Website: www.acbanet.org

Bay Area Legal Aid
Primary Address: 405 14th St., Fl 9
City: Oakland
State: CA
Zip Code: 94612
General Phone: 510-663-4751
Fax: 510-663-4711
Counties Served: Alameda, Contra Costa, Marin, Napa, San Francisco, San Mateo, Santa Clara
Case Types: Domestic Violence, Housing, Public Benefits
Case Restrictions: Low-income
Website: www.baylegal.org

Bay Area Legal Aid Alameda Regional Office
Primary Address: 405 14th Street, 11th Floor
City: Oakland
State: CA
Zip Code: 94612
General Phone: 510-663-4755
Intake Phone: 800-551-5554
Counties Served: Alameda, Contra Costa, San

Francisco, San Mateo, Santa Clara
Case Types: Domestic Violence, Housing, Public Benefits
Case Restrictions: Low-income
Website: www.baylegal.org

Bay Area Legal Aid Contra Costa Regional Office
Primary Address: 1017 Macdonald Avenue
City: Richmond
State: CA
Zip Code: 94801
General Phone: 510-233-9954
Counties Served: Contra Costa
Case Types: Domestic Violence, Housing, Public Benefits
Case Restrictions: Low-income
Website: www.baylegal.org

Bay Area Legal Aid Marin/Napa Regional Office
Primary Address: 30 North San Pedro Road, Ste 250
City: San Rafael
State: CA
Zip Code: 94903
General Phone: 415-479-8224
Counties Served: Marin
Case Types: Domestic Violence, Housing, Public Benefits
Case Restrictions: Low-income
Website: www.baylegal.org

Bay Area Legal Aid Pittsburg Office
Primary Address: 1901 Railroad Avenue, Ste D
City: Pittsburg
State: CA
Zip Code: 94565
General Phone: 925-432-1123
Counties Served: Contra Costa
Case Types: Domestic Violence, Housing, Public Benefits
Case Restrictions: Low-income
Website: www.baylegal.org

Bay Area Legal Aid San Francisco Regional Office
Primary Address: 50 Fell Street, 1st Fl
City: San Francisco
State: CA
Zip Code: 94102
General Phone: 415-982-1300
Counties Served: San Francisco
Case Types: Domestic Violence, Housing, Public Benefits

Case Restrictions: Low-income
Website: www.baylegal.org

Bay Area Legal Aid San Mateo Regional Office
Primary Address: 2287 El Camino Real
City: San Mateo
State: CA
Zip Code: 94403
General Phone: 650-358-0745
Counties Served: San Mateo
Case Types: Domestic Violence, Housing, Public Benefits
Case Restrictions: Low-income
Website: www.baylegal.org

Bay Area Legal Aid Santa Clara Regional Office
Primary Address: 2 West Santa Clara Street, 8th Floor
City: San Jose
State: CA
Zip Code: 95113
General Phone: 408-283-3700
Counties Served: Santa Clara
Case Types: Domestic Violence, Housing, Public Benefits
Case Restrictions: Low-income
Website: www.baylegal.org

East Bay Community Law Center
Primary Address: 3130 Shattuck Ave.
City: Berkeley
State: CA
Zip Code: 94705-1823
General Phone: 510-548-4040
Fax: 510-548-2566
Intake Phone: 510-548-4040
Counties Served: Alameda
Case Types: AIDS/HIV, Community Economic Development, Health, Immigration, Public Benefits, Wills
Case Restrictions: Certain services are restricted to people living with HIV; otherwise, LSC financial eligibility guidelines generally apply.
Website: www.ebclc.org
Organization Email: info@ebclc.org

Family Violence Law Center
Primary Address: P.O. Box 22009
City: Oakland
State: CA
Zip Code: 94623
General Phone: 510-208-0220
Fax: 510-540-5373

Intake Phone: 510-540-5370
Counties Served: Alameda
Case Types: Child Custody, Dissolution of Marriage, Domestic Violence, Elder Law, Housing, Immigration, Public Benefits, Termination of Parental Rights
Case Restrictions: Clients must have domestic violence case/issue to receive other legal/social services.

Legal Assistance for Seniors
Primary Address: 614 Grand Ave., Ste 400
City: Oakland
State: CA
Zip Code: 94610-3523
General Phone: 510-832-3040
Fax: 510-987-7399
Intake Phone: 510-832-3040
Counties Served: Alameda
Case Types: Consumer, Domestic Violence, Elder Law, Health, Housing, Immigration, Public Benefits
Other Case Types: Guardianship, Elder Law Conservatorship
Case Restrictions: Must be 60 years of age or older.

BWA-Legal Advocacy Program
Primary Address: P.O. Box 6556
City: Concord
State: CA
Zip Code: 94524-1556
General Phone: 925-676-3122
Fax: 925-676-0564
Intake Phone: 925-676-3122
Counties Served: Contra Costa
Case Types: Child Custody, Dissolution of Marriage, Domestic Violence
Case Restrictions: Family law issues

Contra Costa Senior Legal Services
Primary Address: 4006 MacDonald Ave.
City: Richmond
State: CA
Zip Code: 94805
General Phone: 510-374-3712
Fax: 510-374-3304
Intake Phone: 510-374-3712
Counties Served: Contra Costa
Case Types: Consumer, Elder Law, Housing, Individual Rights, Public Benefits, Wills
Other Case Types: Elder Abuse
Case Restrictions: Client must be 60 and resident of Contra Costa County.
Website: www.seniorlegalservices.org

**Central California Legal Services Inc. —
Voluntary Legal Services Program**
Primary Address: 1999 Tuolumne Street 700
City: Fresno
State: CA
Zip Code: 93721
General Phone: 559-570-1200
Fax: 559-570-1254
Intake Phone: 559-570-1200
Counties Served: Fresno, Kings, Mariposa,
Merced, Tulare, Tuolumne
Case Types: Bankruptcy, Community Economic
Development, Consumer, Child Custody,
Domestic Violence, Education, Elder Law,
Employment, Health, Housing, Immigration,
Public Benefits, Real Estate, Wills
Other Case Types: Conservatorships,
Guardianships, Domestic Violence
Restraining Orders
Case Restrictions: Financial eligibility &
citizenship/LPR.
Website: www.centralcallegal.org
Organization Email: fresno@centralcallegal.org

Humboldt County Bar Association
Primary Address: P.O. Box 1017
City: Eureka
State: CA
Zip Code: 95502-1017
General Phone: 707-445-2652
Fax: 707-445-0935
Counties Served: Humboldt
Case Types: Consumer, Health, Housing, Real
Estate, Torts, Wills

Humboldt Legal Center
Primary Address: Humboldt State University
City: Arcata
State: CA
Zip Code: 95521
General Phone: 707-826-3824
Intake Phone: 707-826-3824
Counties Served: Humboldt
Case Types: Adoption, Child Custody,
Dissolution of Marriage, Domestic Violence,
Housing, Termination of Parental Rights,
Wills
Case Restrictions: No criminal matters

North Coast AIDS Project
Primary Address: 529 I St.
City: Eureka
State: CA
Zip Code: 95501
General Phone: 707-268-2132

Fax: 707-445-6097
Intake Phone: 707-268-2132
Counties Served: Del Norte, Humboldt
Case Types: AIDS/HIV
Other Case Types: File for do not resuscitate,
etc., power of attorney, worker's comp.
Case Restrictions: Must be HIV+

**Asian Pacific American Legal Center of
Southern California**
Primary Address: 1145 Wilshire Blvd Fl 2
City: Los Angeles
State: CA
Zip Code: 90015
General Phone: 213-977-7500
Fax: 213-977-7595
Case Types: Consumer, Child Custody,
Dissolution of Marriage, Domestic Violence,
Employment, Health, Housing, Immigration,
Public Benefits
Case Restrictions: Language capability, no class-
action for civil rights cases, conflict of interest.
Email: www.apalc@earthlink.net

Bet Tzedek Legal Services
Primary Address: 145 S Fairfax Ave., 200
City: Los Angeles
State: CA
Zip Code: 90036-2166
General Phone: 323-939-0506
Fax: 323-939-1040
Counties Served: Los Angeles
Case Types: AIDS/HIV, Adoption, Bankruptcy,
Consumer, Elder Law, Employment, Housing,
Public Benefits, Real Estate, Wills
Other Case Types: Employment rights, Care-
giver issues
Case Restrictions: Clients must be residents of
LA county, all must be prescreened prior to
being given appointment, case must have merit.
Website: www.bettzedek.org

Break the Cycle
Primary Address: P.O. Box 64996
City: Los Angeles
State: CA
Zip Code: 90064
General Phone: 310-286-3366
Fax: 310-286-3386
Intake Phone: 888-988-8336
Counties Served: Los Angeles
Case Types: Domestic Violence
Other Case Types: Domestic Violence related
cases for Youth Ages 12–22
Case Restrictions: Client must live within the

Los Angeles County and must be within the ages of 12–22 and have experienced Domestic Violence.
Website: www.breakthecycle.org

Burbank Bar Association Lawyer Referral Service and Legal Aid
Primary Address: 2219 W Olive Ave., Ste 100
City: Burbank
State: CA
Zip Code: 91506-2625
General Phone: 818-843-0931
Fax: 818-843-5852
Counties Served: Los Angeles

City of Santa Fe Springs Legal Services Program
Primary Address: 9255 Pioneer Blvd.
City: Santa Fe Springs
State: CA
Zip Code: 90670-2380
General Phone: 562-692-0261
Fax: 562-695-8620
Case Restrictions: Must live in Santa Fe Springs or unincorporated areas of Whittier, the town of Los Neitos, and the city of Pico Rivera.
Organization Email: familyandhumanservices@santafesprings.org

Community Legal Services
Primary Address: 11834 Firestone Blvd.
City: Norwalk
State: CA
Zip Code: 90650-2901
General Phone: 562-864-9935
Fax: 562-863-8853
Intake Phone: 800-834-5001
Counties Served: Los Angeles
Case Types: Consumer, Child Custody, Dissolution of Marriage, Domestic Violence, Health, Housing, Individual Rights, Public Benefits
Case Restrictions: We are not able to serve undocumented individuals.

Disability Rights Legal Center
Primary Address: 919 S Albany St.
City: Los Angeles
State: CA
Zip Code: 90015
General Phone: 213-736-1031 (V & TDD)
Fax: 213-736-1428
Intake Phone: 213-736-1334
Counties Served: Kern, Los Angeles, Orange, San Bernadino, San Diego, Ventura

Case Types: Housing, Individual Rights
Other Case Types: Cancer Advocacy, Disability Rights, Special Education
Website: www.disabilityrightslegalcenter.org

El Rescate Legal Services
Primary Address: 1340 S Bonnie Brae St.
City: Los Angeles
State: CA
Zip Code: 90006-5403
General Phone: 213-387-3284
Fax: 213-387-9189
Counties Served: Los Angeles
Case Types: Immigration
Case Restrictions: We do not accept cases of those who persecuted others.

Harriett Buhai Center for Family Law
Primary Address: 3250 Wilshire Blvd., Ste 710
City: Los Angeles
State: CA
Zip Code: 90010
General Phone: 213-388-7505
Fax: 323-939-2199
Intake Phone: 213-388-7515
Counties Served: Los Angeles
Case Types: Child Custody, Dissolution of Marriage, Domestic Violence
Website: www.hbcfl.org

HIV & AIDS Legal Services Alliance, Inc. (HALSA)
Primary Address: 3550 Wilshire Blvd. 750
City: Los Angeles
State: CA
Zip Code: 90010
General Phone: 213-201-1640
Fax: 213-993-1594
Intake Phone: 213-201-1640
Counties Served: Los Angeles
Case Types: AIDS/HIV, Employment, Health, Housing, Immigration, Individual Rights, Public Benefits, Wills
Other Case Types: Tax form preparation
Case Restrictions: Must be HIV+, low-income, and live in Los Angeles county.
Website: www.halsaservices.org

Immigration Legal Assistance Project
Primary Address: 300 N Los Angeles St., Ste 3107
City: Los Angeles
State: CA
Zip Code: 90012-3335
General Phone: 213-485-1872

Fax: 213-485-0047
Intake Phone: 213-485-1872
Counties Served: Los Angeles
Case Types: AIDS/HIV, Immigration
Website: www.lacba.org

Inner City Law Center
Primary Address: 1325 E 7th St.
City: Los Angeles
State: CA
Zip Code: 90021-1101
General Phone: 213-891-2880
Fax: 213-891-2888
Intake Phone: 213-891-2880
Counties Served: Los Angeles
Case Types: Housing, Public Benefits

Legal Aid Foundation of Los Angeles
Primary Address: 1102 Crenshaw Blvd.
City: Los Angeles
State: CA
Zip Code: 90019-3111
General Phone: 323-801-7924
Fax: 323-801-7945
Intake Phone: 800-399-4529
Counties Served: Los Angeles
Case Types: Community Economic
Development, Consumer, Child Custody,
Dissolution of Marriage, Domestic Violence,
Employment, Health, Housing, Immigration,
Individual Rights, Public Benefits, Real Estate,
Termination of Parental Rights, Torts
Case Restrictions: Cannot serve undocumented
aliens.

**Legal Services Program for Pasadena and San
Gabriel-Pomona Valley**
Primary Address: 243 W Mission Blvd., Ste 303
City: Pomona
State: CA
Zip Code: 91766-1560
General Phone: 909-622-7455
Fax: 909-469-1729
Intake Phone: 909-622-1417
Counties Served: Los Angeles
Case Types: Bankruptcy, Child Custody,
Dissolution of Marriage, Domestic Violence
Other Case Types: Post-decree modifications of
custody/visitation
Case Restrictions: Must reside in service area;
jurisdiction over case must be either close to a
volunteer attorney or be accepted for represen-
tation by a Legal Aid/Legal Service program in
a foreign jurisdiction.

Los Angeles Center for Law and Justice
Primary Address: 2606 E 1st St.
City: Los Angeles
State: CA
Zip Code: 90033-3506
General Phone: 213-266-2690
Fax: 213-266-2695
Counties Served: Los Angeles
Case Types: Consumer, Dissolution of
Marriage, Domestic Violence, Housing,
Public Benefits, Real Estate
Case Restrictions: Must live in service areas:
90031, 90032, 90033, 90041, 90042, 90063,
90065, 90023, 90039 (Atwater only)

**Los Angeles County Bar Association
Barristers AIDS Legal Services Project**
Primary Address: P.O. Box 55020
City: Los Angeles
State: CA
Zip Code: 90055-2020
General Phone: 213-896-6436
Fax: 213-896-6500
Counties Served: Los Angeles
Case Types: AIDS/HIV

**Los Angeles County Bar Association
Barristers Domestic Violence Project**
Primary Address: 261 S Figueroa St.
City: Los Angeles
State: CA
Zip Code: 90014-1648
General Phone: 213-896-6491
Fax: 213-896-6500
Intake Phone: 213-624-3665
Counties Served: Los Angeles
Case Types: Domestic Violence
Website: lacba.org

Los Angeles Free Clinic
Primary Address: 8405 Beverly Blvd.
City: Los Angeles
State: CA
Zip Code: 90048-3401
General Phone: 323-653-8622 (Admin.)
Fax: 323-658-6773
Intake Phone: 323-655-2697
Case Types: Bankruptcy, Dissolution of
Marriage, Immigration, Juvenile
Other Case Types: Response To Summons.
Case Restrictions: No property may be
involved, and clients are assisted with uncon-
tested simple divorce only.

Los Angeles Gay and Lesbian Center Legal Services Department
Primary Address: 1625 Schrader Blvd.
City: Los Angeles
State: CA
Zip Code: 90028-6213
General Phone: 213-993-7670
Fax: 213-933-7699
Counties Served: Los Angeles
Case Types: Child Custody, Dissolution of Marriage, Domestic Violence, Housing, Immigration, Individual Rights, Wills

Neighborhood Legal Services of Los Angeles County
Primary Address: 13327 Van Nuys Blvd.
City: Pacoima
State: CA
Zip Code: 91331-3099
General Phone: 818-896-5211
Fax: 818-896-6647
Intake Phone: 800-433-6251
Counties Served: Los Angeles
Case Types: Community Economic Development, Consumer, Child Custody, Dissolution of Marriage, Domestic Violence, Education, Employment, Health, Housing, Immigration, Individual Rights, Juvenile, Public Benefits, Termination of Parental Rights
Other Case Types: Discrimination, Family Law, Community Legal Education
Case Restrictions: NLS is subject to the Legal Service Corporation (LSC) guidelines on financial and alien eligibility.
Website: www.nls-la.org
Organization Email: nls@nls-la.org

Pasadena Human Services Department Consumer Action Center
Primary Address: 1020 N Fair Oaks Ave.
City: Pasadena
State: CA
Zip Code: 91103-3011
General Phone: 626-744-7300
Fax: 626-798-5834
Counties Served: Los Angeles
Case Types: Consumer, Domestic Violence, Housing, Public Benefits

Police Watch — Police Misconduct Lawyer Referral Service
Primary Address: 611 S Catalina St.
City: Los Angeles
State: CA
Zip Code: 90005-1730

General Phone: 213-387-3435
Fax: 213-387-9085
Intake Phone: 213-387-3325
Counties Served: Kern, Los Angeles, Orange, Riverside, San Bernardino, San Diego, Ventura
Case Types: Individual Rights
Other Case Types: Police Misconduct, Civil Rights Violations.
Case Restrictions: No restrictions: we accept cases regarding police misconduct. No fees charged for case acceptance.

Public Counsel Law Center
Primary Address: 601 S Ardmore Ave.
City: Los Angeles
State: CA
Zip Code: 90005-2323
General Phone: 213-385-2977
Fax: 213-385-9089
Counties Served: Los Angeles
Case Types: Adoption, Bankruptcy, Community Economic Development, Consumer, Domestic Violence, Education, Elder Law, Health, Housing, Immigration, Juvenile, Public Benefits, Real Estate, Termination of Parental Rights, Torts, Wills
Other Case Types: School expulsion, SIJS, VAWA, Transactional, Contracts, Expungments, Zoning, Land Use, Tax, Notary Fraud, Auto Fraud, Guardian Ad Litem and Guardianship.
Case Restrictions: Financial eligibility (at or below the federal income guidelines). We do not take criminal cases.
Website: www.publiccounsel.org
Organization Email: web@publiccounsel.org

San Fernando Valley Bar Association LRIS
Primary Address: 21300 Oxnard St., Ste 250
City: Woodland Hills
State: CA
Zip Code: 91367
General Phone: 818-227-0490
Fax: 818-227-0499
Intake Phone: 818-340-4529
Counties Served: Los Angeles, Ventura
Case Types: AIDS/HIV, Adoption, Bankruptcy, Community Economic Development, Consumer, Child Custody, Domestic Violence, Education, Elder Law, Employment, Health, Housing, Immigration, Individual Rights, Juvenile, Public Benefits, Real Estate, Termination of Parental Rights, Torts, Wills
Website: www.sfvba.org/needalawyer.htm

Legal Aid of Marin County
Primary Address: 30 N San Pedro Rd. 220
City: San Rafael
State: CA
Zip Code: 94903
General Phone: 415-492-0230
Fax: 415-492-0947
Intake Phone: 800-498-7666
Counties Served: Marin
Case Types: Bankruptcy, Consumer, Domestic Violence, Employment, Health, Housing, Immigration, Individual Rights, Juvenile, Real Estate, Termination of Parental Rights, Torts, Wills
Case Restrictions: financial eligibility, county residency.
Website: www.legalaidmarin.org
Organization Email: justice@legal-aid.marin.ca.us

Legal Services of Northern California
Primary Address: 421 N Oak St.
City: Ukiah
State: CA
Zip Code: 95482-4303
General Phone: 707-462-1471
Fax: 707-462-9483
Intake Phone: 877-529-7700
Counties Served: Lake, Mendocino
Case Types: Community Economic Development, Consumer, Health, Housing, Public Benefits
Case Restrictions: LSC restrictions
Website: lsnc.net
Organization Email: ukiah-office@lsnc.net

Central California Legal Services
Primary Address: 357 W Main St., Ste 201
City: Merced
State: CA
Zip Code: 95340
General Phone: 209-723-5466
Fax: 559-723-1315
Counties Served: Mariposa, Merced, Tuolumne
Case Types: Bankruptcy
Other Case Types: Low-income tax problems
Case Restrictions: We are restricted to serving only those who qualify for services under LSC guidelines. They must be low income and a U.S. Citizen or lawful permanent resident.
Website: www.centralcallegal.org

Mono County Bar Association Legal Advice and Referral Clinic
Primary Address: P.O. Box 3337
City: Mammoth Lakes
State: CA
Zip Code: 93546-3337
General Phone: 760-934-4558
Fax: 760-934-2530
Counties Served: Mono
Case Types: Consumer, Dissolution of Marriage, Domestic Violence, Housing, Individual Rights

Legal Aid of the Central Coast Pro Bono Program of Monterey County
Primary Address: 2100 Garden Rd., Bldg B
City: Monterey
State: CA
Zip Code: 93940-5366
General Phone: 408-375-0505 (Monterey)
Fax: 408-375-0501
Counties Served: Monterey
Case Restrictions: Must be a U.S. citizen or legal resident.
Organization Email: itdept@crla.org

Nevada County Lawyer Referral Service
Primary Address: 714 W Main St., Fl 9
City: Nevada City
State: CA
Zip Code: 95959
General Phone: 530-265-4129
Fax: 530-265-4139
Counties Served: Nevada
Case Types: Adoption, Bankruptcy, Consumer, Child Custody, Dissolution of Marriage, Elder Law, Employment, Real Estate, Torts, Wills

Public Law Center
Primary Address: 601 Civic Center Drive West
City: Santa Ana
State: CA
Zip Code: 92701-4002
General Phone: 714-541-1010
Fax: 714-541-5157
Counties Served: Orange
Case Types: Adoption, Bankruptcy, Community Economic Development, Consumer, Child Custody, Dissolution of Marriage, Domestic Violence, Elder Law, Housing, Immigration, Real Estate, Torts, Wills
Case Restrictions: Clients must meet California IOLTA program income eligibility requirements (75% of HUD "low income" figure for county).
Website: www.publiclawcenter.org

Legal Services of Northern California Mother Lode Office-VLSP
Primary Address: 190 Reamer St.
City: Auburn
State: CA
Zip Code: 95603-4721
General Phone: 530-823-7560
Fax: 530-823-7601
Counties Served: Amador, Calaveras, El Dorado, Nevada, Placer, Sierra
Case Types: AIDS/HIV, Consumer, Child Custody, Dissolution of Marriage, Elder Law, Housing, Individual Rights, Public Benefits, Wills
Other Case Types: Health

Desert AIDS Project Legal Services
Primary Address: 750 South Vella Road
City: Palm Springs
State: CA
Zip Code: 92264
General Phone: 619-323-2118
Fax: 619-323-9865
Case Types: AIDS/HIV

Inland Empire Latino Lawyers Association, Inc.
Primary Address: 2060 University Ave., Ste 113
City: Riverside
State: CA
Zip Code: 92507-5210
General Phone: 951-369-3009
Fax: 951-369-6211
Intake Phone: 951-369-3009
Counties Served: Riverside, San Bernardino
Case Types: Consumer, Child Custody, Dissolution of Marriage, Domestic Violence, Housing, Individual Rights, Termination of Parental Rights, Torts
Other Case Types: Educate teen parents and pregnant minors on issues re: custody/visitation, child support, establish paternity, TRO.
Case Restrictions: Program utilizes the LSC Income Eligibility Guidelines set at 125% of poverty, up to a maximum of 150% of the guidelines. IELLA provides service to legal and non-legal residents.
Website: www.iellaaid.org
Organization Email: iellaaid@aol.com

Riverside County Bar Association Public Service Law Corp.
Primary Address: 4129 Main St., Ste 101
City: Riverside
State: CA
Zip Code: 92501-3628
General Phone: 909-682-5213 (Admin.)
Fax: 909-682-0106
Intake Phone: 909-682-7968
Counties Served: Riverside
Case Types: Adoption, Consumer, Child Custody, Dissolution of Marriage, Domestic Violence, Housing, Real Estate, Torts, Wills
Other Case Types: Guardianships

Voluntary Legal Services Program of Northern California, Inc.
Primary Address: 517 12th Street
City: Sacramento
State: CA
Zip Code: 95814-1418
General Phone: 916-551-2116
Fax: 916-551-2120
Intake Phone: 916-551-2102
Counties Served: El Dorado, Placer, Sacramento, San Joaquin, Yolo
Case Types: Bankruptcy, Consumer, Housing, Public Benefits, Torts
Other Case Types: Conservatorships, Criminal Records Expungement, Debt Collection Defense, Estate Planning, Guardianships, Landlord/Tenant, Probate
Case Restrictions: All LSC restrictions
Website: www.vlsp.org

Women Escaping A Violent Environment - WEAVE
Primary Address: 1900 K St.
City: Sacramento
State: CA
Zip Code: 95814-4107
General Phone: 916-448-2321
Fax: 916-448-0270
Intake Phone: 916-448-2321
Counties Served: Sacramento
Case Types: Domestic Violence
Case Restrictions: Must be a victim of domestic violence.

Legal Aid Clinic of Redlands
Primary Address: 16 E Olive Ave.
City: Redlands
State: CA
Zip Code: 92373-5248
General Phone: 909-792-2762
Fax: 909-793-8788
Counties Served: San Bernardino
Case Types: Bankruptcy, Child Custody, Dissolution of Marriage, Domestic Violence, Elder Law, Termination of Parental Rights

Case Restrictions: Must be a resident of San Bernadino.

Legal Aid Society of San Bernardino Inc
Primary Address: 354 W Sixth St.
City: San Bernardino
State: CA
Zip Code: 92401-1201
General Phone: 909-889-7328
Fax: 909-889-6338
Counties Served: San Bernardino
Case Types: Child Custody, Dissolution of Marriage, Domestic Violence, Housing
Case Restrictions: LSC restrictions

Center for Community Solutions Domestic Violence Legal Clinic
Primary Address: 4508 Mission Bay Dr.
City: San Diego
State: CA
Zip Code: 92109-4919
General Phone: 619-272-5328
Fax: 619-272-5361
Counties Served: San Diego
Case Types: Child Custody, Dissolution of Marriage, Domestic Violence
Case Restrictions: Must pertain to domestic violence.
Organization Email: info@ccssd.org

Elder Law & Advocacy Senior Citizens Legal Services
Primary Address: 3675 Ruffin Road 315
City: San Diego
State: CA
Zip Code: 92123
General Phone: 858-565-1392
Fax: 858-565-1394
Intake Phone: 858-565-1392
Counties Served: Imperial, San Diego
Case Types: Elder Law
Other Case Types: General Civil, elder abuse, nursing home.
Case Restrictions: No criminal matters.
Website: seniorlaw-sd.org

San Diego Volunteer Lawyer Program
Primary Address: 625 Broadway, Ste 925
City: San Diego
State: CA
Zip Code: 92101-5499
General Phone: 619-235-5656
Fax: 619-235-5668
Intake Phone: 619-235-5656
Counties Served: San Diego

Case Types: Child Custody, Dissolution of Marriage, Domestic Violence, Education, Elder Law, Health, Immigration, Individual Rights, Wills
Other Case Types: Family law mediation, guardianship.
Case Restrictions: Applicant must be financially eligible for assistance.
Website: www.sdvlp.org

San Diego Volunteer Lawyer Program AIDS Law Team
Primary Address: 625 Broadway, Ste 925
City: San Diego
State: CA
Zip Code: 92101-5499
General Phone: 619-235-5656 ext. 105
Fax: 619-235-5668
Counties Served: San Diego
Case Types: Bankruptcy, Dissolution of Marriage, Domestic Violence, Housing, Individual Rights, Public Benefits, Wills
Other Case Types: HIV/AIDS issues
Case Restrictions: Clients have to prove by medical records that they are HIV positive.
Website: www.sdvlp.org

AIDS Legal Referral Panel of the San Francisco Bay Area
Primary Address: 582 Market St.
City: San Francisco
State: CA
Zip Code: 94104-5310
General Phone: 415-291-5454
Fax: 415-291-5833
Case Types: AIDS/HIV, Adoption, Bankruptcy, Consumer, Child Custody, Dissolution of Marriage, Employment, Health, Housing, Individual Rights, Public Benefits, Real Estate, Termination of Parental Rights, Torts, Wills
Case Restrictions: HIV+ or HIV related legal issue.
Website: www.alrp.org

API Legal Outreach
Primary Address: 1188 Franklin St., Ste 202
City: San Francisco
State: CA
Zip Code: 94109-6852
General Phone: 415-567-6255
Fax: 415-567-6248
Counties Served: Alameda, San Francisco, San Mateo
Case Types: Consumer, Child Custody, Dissolution of Marriage, Domestic Violence,

Individual Rights, Public Benefits, Wills
Other Case Types: Elder Abuse

Cooperative Restraining Order Clinic
Primary Address: 3543 - 18th Street, 3rd Floor,
Box #5
City: San Francisco
State: CA
Zip Code: 94110
General Phone: 415-864-1790
Fax: 415-241-9491
Intake Phone: 415-252-2844
Counties Served: San Francisco
Case Types: Domestic Violence
Organization Email: roclinic@aol.com

**Lawyers' Committee for Civil Rights Legal
Services for Entrepreneurs**
Primary Address: 131 Stewart Street, 400
City: San Francisco
State: CA
Zip Code: 94117
General Phone: 415-543-9444
Fax: 415-543-0296
Intake Phone: 415-543-9444
Counties Served: Alameda, Contra Costa, San
Francisco
Case Types: Community Economic
Development
Other Case Types: Legal Services for
Entrepreneurs provides free business legal
services to: low-income individuals, including
women and persons of color, who want to
start or develop businesses.
Case Restrictions: When reviewing an applica-
tion for services, LSE will consider both the
individual and his/her business's impact on
the surrounding community. LSE will provide
services to higher income applicants only
under certain circumstances.
Organization Email: helen@lcc.r.com

**Lawyers' Committee Civil Rights of the San
Francisco Bay Area**
Primary Address: 301 Mission St Ste 400
City: San Francisco
State: CA
Zip Code: 94105-2258
General Phone: 415-543-9444
Fax: 415-543-0296
Counties Served: San Francisco
Case Types: Community Economic
Development, Consumer, Education,
Housing, Individual Rights

Other Case Types: Asylum
Case Restrictions: Must be low-income.

Legal Services for Children
Primary Address: 1254 Market St., Fl 3
City: San Francisco
State: CA
Zip Code: 94102-4801
General Phone: 415-863-3762
Fax: 415-863-7708
Intake Phone: 415-863-3762
Counties Served: Alameda, Contra Costa,
Marin, Napa, San Francisco, San Mateo,
Santa Clara, Solano, Sonoma
Case Types: AIDS/HIV, Education, Juvenile
Other Case Types: Guardianship
Case Restrictions: Our office only represents
minors.

**Volunteer Legal Services Program of the Bar
Association of San Francisco**
Primary Address: 301 Battery Street, 3rd Floor
City: San Francisco
State: CA
Zip Code: 94111
General Phone: 415-982-1600
Fax: 415-477-2390
Intake Phone: 415-989-1616
Counties Served: Alameda, Contra Costa,
Marin, San Francisco, San Mateo, Santa Clara
Case Types: Adoption, Bankruptcy,
Community Economic Development,
Consumer, Child Custody, Dissolution of
Marriage, Domestic Violence, Elder Law,
Health, Housing, Immigration, Individual
Rights, Public Benefits, Torts, Wills
Other Case Types: Homelessness, SSI issues
Case Restrictions: Financial eligibility largely
based on state definition of low income
but varies by project; ability to work with
volunteers.
Website: www.sfbar.org/vlsp

**Workers' Rights Clinic Employment Law
Center**
Primary Address: 1663 Mission St., Ste 400
City: San Francisco
State: CA
Zip Code: 94103-2449
General Phone: 415-864-8848
Fax: 415-864-8199
Intake Phone: 415-864-8208
Counties Served: Alameda, Contra Costa, San
Mateo, Marin, Santa Clara, Sonoma, San
Francisco

Case Types: Employment
Website: employmentlawcenter.org

Community Services AIDS Program
Primary Address: 1601 East Hazelton Avenue
City: Stockton
State: CA
Zip Code: 95201-2009
General Phone: 209-468-2235
Fax: 209-468-3495
Case Types: AIDS/HIV

San Luis Obispo Legal Alternatives Corporation
Primary Address: 1160 Marsh St., Ste 114
City: San Luis Obispo
State: CA
Zip Code: 93401-3377
General Phone: 805-544-7997 (Admin.)
Fax: 805-544-3904
Intake Phone: 805-544-7995
Counties Served: San Luis Obispo
Case Types: Adoption, Bankruptcy, Consumer, Domestic Violence, Elder Law, Housing, Public Benefits, Real Estate, Torts, Wills

Legal Aid Society of San Mateo County
Primary Address: 521 East 5th Ave.
City: San Mateo
State: CA
Zip Code: 94402
General Phone: 650-558-0915
Fax: 650-558-0673
Intake Phone: 650-558-0915
Counties Served: San Mateo
Case Types: Consumer, Education, Elder Law, Health, Housing
Other Case Types: Assistance for Seniors, Conservatorships, Guardianships, Special Education and General Civil Litigation Referral
Case Restrictions: Low-Income
Website: www.legalaidsmc.org

Stanford Community Law Clinic
Primary Address: 2117 University Avenue, Suite A
City: East Palo Alto
State: CA
Zip Code: 94303
General Phone: 650-475-0560
Fax: 650-326-4162
Counties Served: San Mateo, Santa Clara
Case Types: Employment, Housing
Case Restrictions: LSC guidelines
Website: www.law.stanford.edu/clinics/sclc/

Legal Aid of North Bay Private Attorney Involvement Program
Primary Address: 1227 Coombs St.
City: Napa
State: CA
Zip Code: 94559-2539
General Phone: 707-255-4933
Fax: 707-255-2312
Intake Phone: 800-498-7666
Counties Served: Napa, Marin
Case Types: AIDS/HIV, Adoption, Bankruptcy, Community Economic Development, Consumer, Child Custody, Dissolution of Marriage, Domestic Violence, Education, Elder Law, Employment, Health, Housing, Immigration, Individual Rights, Juvenile, Public Benefits, Real Estate, Termination of Parental Rights, Torts, Wills
Case Restrictions: Residence in Marin or Napa counties
Organization Email: justice@legal-aid.marin.ca.us

AIDS Legal Services
Primary Address: 111 W Saint John St., Ste 315
City: San Jose
State: CA
Zip Code: 95113-1104
General Phone: 408-293-3135
Fax: 408-293-0106
Counties Served: Santa Clara
Case Types: AIDS/HIV, Bankruptcy, Consumer, Child Custody, Dissolution of Marriage, Housing, Individual Rights, Public Benefits, Real Estate, Torts, Wills
Case Restrictions: Must be HIV/AIDS positive.

Next Door Solutions to Domestic Violence Legal Advocacy Program
Primary Address: 1181 N 4th St.
City: San Jose
State: CA
Zip Code: 95112-4945
General Phone: 408-279-7550
Fax: 408-279-7562
Intake Phone: 408-279-7550
Counties Served: Santa Clara
Case Types: Domestic Violence
Case Restrictions: Client must be a victim of domestic violence.

Pro Bono Project of Silicon Valley
Primary Address: 480 N 1st St., Ste 219
City: San Jose
State: CA

Zip Code: 95112-4040
General Phone: 408-998-5298
Fax: 408-971-9672
Intake Phone: 408-998-5298
Counties Served: Santa Clara
Case Types: Adoption, Bankruptcy, Consumer,
Child Custody, Dissolution of Marriage,
Domestic Violence, Education, Elder Law,
Employment, Health, Housing, Immigration,
Individual Rights, Juvenile, Real Estate, Torts

Public Interest Law Firm
Primary Address: 111 W Saint John St., Ste
315
City: San Jose
State: CA
Zip Code: 95113-1104
General Phone: 408-293-4790
Fax: 408-293-0106
Counties Served: Santa Clara
Case Types: AIDS/HIV, Consumer, Education,
Elder Law, Employment, Health, Housing,
Immigration, Individual Rights, Juvenile,
Public Benefits, Torts
Case Restrictions: No class action and/or
impact litigation

**Support Network for Battered Women Legal
Program**
Primary Address: 444 Castro St., Ste 305
City: Mountain View
State: CA
Zip Code: 94041-2051
General Phone: 650-940-7860
Fax: 650-940-4382
Intake Phone: 800-572-2782
Counties Served: Santa Clara
Case Types: Child Custody, Dissolution of
Marriage, Domestic Violence
Case Restrictions: Must reside in Santa Clara
County
Website: www.snbw.org

California Rural Legal Assistance
Primary Address: 21 Carr St.
City: Watsonville
State: CA
Zip Code: 95076-4705
General Phone: 831-724-2253
Fax: 831-724-7530
Counties Served: Monterey, Santa Cruz
Case Types: Bankruptcy, Domestic Violence,
Education, Housing, Public Benefits
Website: www.crla.org
Organization Email: itdept@crla.org

**Legal Services of Northern California Solano
County Office**
Primary Address: 1810 Capitol St.
City: Vallejo
State: CA
Zip Code: 94590-5721
General Phone: 707-643-0054
Fax: 707-643-0144
Intake Phone: 707-643-0054
Counties Served: Solano
Case Types: Community Economic
Development, Consumer, Dissolution of
Marriage, Domestic Violence, Education,
Elder Law, Employment, Health, Housing,
Individual Rights, Public Benefits
Case Restrictions: We follow legal services
corporation client eligibility guidelines and
restrictions.
Website: lsnc.net

Sonoma County Legal Aid
Primary Address: 37 Old Courthouse Sq. 100
City: Santa Rosa
State: CA
Zip Code: 95404-4033
General Phone: 707-542-1290
Fax: 707-542-1195
Intake Phone: 707-542-1290
Counties Served: Sonoma
Case Types: Consumer, Child Custody,
Dissolution of Marriage, Domestic Violence,
Housing

Case Restrictions: Various programs have certain restrictions. Our Self Help Access Center
sees only low-income clients at poverty level or
below. Our Legal Services Referral Project sees
only welfare to work clients. We do information and referral for everyone.
Organization Email: sclapt@sonic.net

Sonoma County Legal Services Foundation
Primary Address: 1212 4th St., Fl 1
City: Santa Rosa
State: CA
Zip Code: 95404-4039
General Phone: 707-546-2924
Fax: 707-546-0263
Intake Phone: 707-546-2924
Counties Served: Sonoma
Case Types: Bankruptcy, Consumer, Child
Custody, Domestic Violence, Employment,
Housing, Juvenile, Wills

California Rural Legal Assistance
Primary Address: 801 15th St., Ste 11
City: Modesto
State: CA
Zip Code: 95354-1132
General Phone: 209-577-3811
Fax: 209-577-1098
Case Types: Education, Elder Law,
Employment, Housing, Individual Rights,
Public Benefits
Case Restrictions: LSC restrictions
Website: www.crla.org

Haven Women's Center
Primary Address: 619 13th St., Fl 1
City: Modesto
State: CA
Zip Code: 95354-2435
General Phone: 209-524-4331
Fax: 209-424-2045
Counties Served: Stanislaus
Case Types: Child Custody, Domestic Violence
Case Restrictions: Client must be a victim of
domestic violence or sexual assault and seeking
protection from her perpetrator.

AIDS Care Legal Clinic
Primary Address: 632 E Thompson Blvd.
City: Ventura
State: CA
Zip Code: 93001
General Phone: 805-643-0446
Fax: 805-643-9474
Intake Phone: 805-643-0446
Counties Served: Ventura
Case Types: AIDS/HIV, Bankruptcy,
Consumer, Individual Rights, Wills
Case Restrictions: Must either be a client or the
family member of one of the agency's clients.

Conejo Free Clinic Legal Services
Primary Address: 80 E Hillcrest Dr., Ste 211
City: Thousand Oaks
State: CA
Zip Code: 91360-7881
General Phone: 805-497-3575
Fax: 805-497-4099
Counties Served: Ventura
Case Types: Adoption, Bankruptcy, Consumer,
Child Custody, Dissolution of Marriage,
Domestic Violence, Elder Law, Employment,
Health, Housing, Immigration, Individual
Rights, Juvenile, Real Estate, Termination of
Parental Rights

Grey Law of Ventura County
Primary Address: 290 Maple Ct., Ste 128
City: Ventura
State: CA
Zip Code: 93003-3521
General Phone: 805-658-2266
Fax: 805-658-6339
Counties Served: Ventura
Case Types: Elder Law
Case Restrictions: 60+ years of age and Ventura
county resident

**Ventura County Bar Association Volunteer
Legal Service Program**
Primary Address: 4475 Market St., Suite B
City: Ventura
State: CA
Zip Code: 93003-8051
General Phone: 805-650-7599
Fax: 805-650-8059
Intake Phone: 805-650-7599
Counties Served: Ventura
Case Types: Consumer, Child Custody,
Dissolution of Marriage, Domestic Violence,
Housing
Case Restrictions: Federal poverty guidelines.
Website: www.vcba.org
Organization Email: bar@vcba.org

Central California Legal Services
Primary Address: 208 W Main St., U-1
City: Visalia
State: CA
Zip Code: 93291
General Phone: 559-733-8770
Fax: 559-635-8096
Counties Served: Kings, Tulare
Case Types: Bankruptcy
Other Case Types: Family Law
Case Restrictions: We are restricted to serving
only those who qualify for services under LSC
guidelines. They must be low-income and a citi-
zen of the U.S. or a lawful permanent resident.
Website: www.centralcallegal.org
Organization Email: visalia@centralcallegal.org

Legal Services of Northern California
Primary Address: 619 North St.
City: Woodland
State: CA
Zip Code: 95695-3237
General Phone: 530-662-1065
Fax: 530-662-7941
Counties Served: Yolo

Case Types: Child Custody, Dissolution of
Marriage

California Rural Legal Assistance
Primary Address: 818 D St.
City: Marysville
State: CA
Zip Code: 95901-5321
General Phone: 530-742-5191 x310
Fax: 530-742-0421
Intake Phone: 530-742-5191
Counties Served: Colusa, Sutter, Yuba
Case Types: Community Economic
Development, Education, Employment,
Health, Housing, Individual Rights, Public
Benefits
Organization Email: itdept@crla.org

Crazy, isn't it? Crazy good. Did you
have any idea all these free money options
even existed? **And that is just the state
of California.**

> Free legal
> services
> abound!

Go research your state and I bet you will be amazed at what
you discover. Free legal services abound!

Law Students

If you need help with your will or a divorce or bankruptcy or
any kind of legal activity that has you a little perplexed, check out
the free and reduced fee legal services in your community.

Did you know that many law schools have pro bono programs?
Law students and their professors eat up pro bono work. They love
it. They want to help people at the grass roots level. And we, the
people, want to be helped without paying an arm and a leg.

The American Bar Association lists 170 law schools that have
pro bono programs. How would you like a Harvard lawyer on your
case? At least a Harvard law student. Maybe Columbia University
School of Law? The most prestigious law schools in the country
offer free and reduced fee legal services.

To see the complete list of law schools that offer public service and pro bono work, visit www.abanet.org/legalservices/probono/lawschools/pb_programs_chart.html. Many of these schools require students to perform public service as a graduation requirement.

Visit www.abanet.org/legalservices/probono/ for all kinds of pro bono information and resources. There is so much info, I could fill up the rest of this book on legal services alone, but we have more to get to still.

Foreclosure Aid

> If you are among those with housing issues, there is help available.

Before we move on to more free money topics though, I have to finish up this chapter with a little more legal aid information. As we all know, our economy is facing unprecedented times. Foreclosures were once a random occurrence and now, sadly, they are all too common. Because of the onslaught of foreclosure nightmares, more people than ever need legal help in this area.

If you are among those with housing issues, there is help available. The Institute for Foreclosure Legal Assistance exists to provide help to Americans losing their homes. Your state probably has an office.

Look up www.foreclosurelegalassistance.org/index.php. Here is a sample listing:

California
Legal Aid Foundation of Los Angeles
Housing and Economic Rights Advocates

Colorado
Colorado Legal Services

District of Columbia
Legal Counsel for the Elderly

Florida
Jacksonville Area Legal Aid
Legal Services of Greater Miami

Georgia
Atlanta Legal Aid Society

Illinois
Legal Assistance Foundation of Metropolitan Chicago

Indiana
Indiana Legal Services Inc.

Iowa
Iowa Legal Aid

Kentucky
Appalachian Research and Defense Fund of Kentucky, Inc.

Louisiana
Southeastern Louisiana Legal Services

Maine
Pine Tree Legal Assistance

Maryland
Legal Aid Bureau of Maryland

Massachusetts
Neighborhood Legal Services, Inc.

Michigan
Legal Services of South Central Michigan

Minnesota
Mid-Minnesota Legal Services

Mississippi
Mississippi Legal Services

Missouri
Legal Services of Eastern Missouri, Inc.

Nevada
Legal Aid Center of Southern Nevada, Inc.

New York
Empire Justice Center
Staten Island Legal Services — Homeowner Defense Project
South Brooklyn Legal Services

North Carolina
Financial Protection Law Center
North Carolina Center for Justice

Ohio
Legal Aid Society of Cleveland
Legal Aid Society of Greater Cincinnati

Oregon
Oregon Law Center

Pennsylvania
Community Legal Services of Philadelphia

Texas
Texas Rio Grande Legal Aid

Virginia
Legal Services of Northern Virginia, Inc.

West Virginia
Mountain State Justice

Washington
Columbia Legal Services

Wisconsin

Legal Aid Society of Milwaukee

By going to www.foreclosurelegalassistance.org/index.php, you can click on any of the legal service offices listed above and you will be linked directly to their sites.

Maybe you personally are not facing foreclosure, but your landlord is. Renters are affected by this crisis, too. Many people are facing eviction — even though they pay their rent — because the landlord is dealing with foreclosure proceedings. If you are in this situation, legal aid is available to you as well.

> There are several services offering foreclosure help.

Hope for Homeowners

There are several services offering foreclosure help. The Homeownership Preservation Foundation has a national hotline dedicated to helping individuals facing foreclosure. You can call 888-995-HOPE.

Their mission as stated on their website is as follows:

> "The Homeownership Preservation Foundation has a single mission: to help homeowners avoid foreclosure. We are an independent nonprofit that provides HUD-approved counselors dedicated to helping homeowners.

> The help we offer is free.

> Our counselors are experts in foreclosure prevention and trained to set up a plan of action designed just for you and your situation. When you talk to us, you won't be judged and you won't pay a dime. That's because we don't

just offer general advice — we help you take action.

Counselors will arm you with education and support that assists you in overcoming immediate financial issues…at no cost to you."

If you are facing foreclosure, give hope a chance. Visit www.995hope.org.

The American Bar Association has foreclosure resources also: Foreclosure tax tips at www.abanet.org/tax/taxtips4u/ ForeclosureTaxTips1.pdf and answers to frequently asked questions (FAQs) about foreclosure are found using the following link: www. abanet.org/rppt/public/realestate/foreclosure.html.

Foreclosures are regulated by state laws, but there are national organizations that offer assistance, advice and guidance:

AARP.org Foreclosure Information = www.aarp.org/money/consumer/

Consumer Action — Avoiding Foreclosure = www.consumeraction.gov/caw_housing_foreclosure.shtml

Federal Trade Commission — Mortgage Info = www.ftc.gov/bcp/edu/pubs/consumer/homes/rea04.shtm

HUD — Find a Housing Counselor = www.hud.gov/ offices/hsg/sfh/hcc/hccprof14.cfm

HUD — General Foreclosure Information = www.hud.gov/foreclosure/index.cfm

HUD — Help for Homeowners Facing the Loss of Their Home = www.hud.gov/offices/hsg/sfh/econ/econ.cfm

HUD — U.S. Department of Housing and Urban Development = www.hud.gov

Housing Policy — Foreclosure and Equity Loss = www.housingpolicy.org/toolbox/strategy/policies/foreclosure_prevention.html

Institute for Foreclosure Legal Assistance = www.foreclosurelegalassistance.org/resources/

LRI Foreclosure Materials = lri.lsc.gov/practice/foreclosure_resources.asp

Legal Services National Technology Assistance Project = lsntap.org/foreclosure_efforts

National Governors Association — State Mortgage Assistance and Refinance Programs = www.nga.org/portal/site/nga/menuitem.9123e83a1f6786440ddcbeeb501010a0/?vgnextoid=aadc799400526110VgnVCM1000001a01010aRCRD

NeighborWorks America = www.nw.org/network/foreclosure/default.asp

NeighborWorks America — Center for Foreclosure Solutions = www.nw.org/network/neighborworksprogs/foreclosuresolutions/default.asp

Pine Tree Legal Services — Foreclosure Prevention Toolkit = www.ptla.org/foreclosure

Self-Help.org Subprime Response = www.self-help.org/about-us/policy-initiatives/subprime-response

(Thanks to source ABA: www.abanet.org/legalservices/findlegalhelp/foreclosuremain.cfm)

To search for local legal resources in your state to help you with foreclosure or other matters, use www.abanet.org/legalservices/findlegalhelp/home.cfm.

In case you were wondering, yes, I could go on and on forever. Isn't it mind-blowing how much free service is available?! Did you have any idea?

Free Advice

Before I wrap up this chapter, one more free resource you need to know (free resource = free money) is www.freeadvice.com. For legal advice, give a click and then narrow it down by your topic:

- ✔ Accidents
- ✔ Bankruptcy
- ✔ Business
- ✔ Criminal
- ✔ Employment
- ✔ Government
- ✔ Injuries and Damages
- ✔ Insurance
- ✔ Intellectual Property
- ✔ Litigation
- ✔ Real Estate
- ✔ Wills, Trusts, and Probate
- ✔ General Practice

FreeAdvice.com is not just for legal advice. (They do have over 600,000 topics in their law section.) They also cover all insurance topics as well.

If you need a place to start, with any problem, free advice is always a good thing.

CHAPTER 16

Foreclosures

It may seem strange, but foreclosures can be a tremendous source of found money. There are so many foreclosure homes, the banks are practically giving them away. The banks don't want them. They are a burden and an expense to the bank's books.

Since this whole mortgage crisis hit, a record number of foreclosures take place every month. Nearly 1.4 million homes have been foreclosed on since July 2007.

If you are in the position to buy, this is a buyers' market! Never before have there been prices like this!

Houses: Cheap

Hold on to your hat, but you can get a house for…$1,000!

Yes, a house for only a grand. I am not making this up. The story was reported by CNN (money.cnn.com/2009/01/08/real_estate/thousand_dollar_homes/index.htm).

In January of 2009, CNNMoney.com did a report on bargain foreclosure properties. By simply pulling up the popular website, www.realtor.com, the reporter searched for homes that had a list selling price for less than $3,000.

Flint, Michigan — 18 houses ; Indianapolis, Indiana — 22; Cleveland, Ohio — 46. In Detroit, Michigan, 709 homes were listed for under $3,000!

Using the website realtor.com, you can find homes in your area, too.

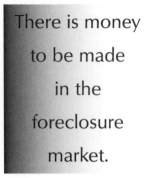

There is money to be made in the foreclosure market.

Most of these homes will need a little maintenance and maybe some fixing up to get ready for resale, or to live in, but even factoring in those repair costs, there is money to be made in the foreclosure market.

The banks just want to unload these homes. There are simply too many and the banks are not making money by holding on to them. You, however, can make lots of money by making smart purchases.

Buy and Flip for $$$

If you can scoop up a house for less than $5,000 and put in another $20,000 in rehab expenses, you can turn around and sell it for twice or three times that price. There are bargains to be had in every state.

Another popular real estate search site to use is www.zillow.com.

The same story reports a home for sale for under $2,000 that had suffered fire damage, but had a nice lot and was in a good area close to downtown. Other homes in that area sold for $100,000. Think about the profit that could come from a small investment in fixing up such a property.

Even if you spent $50,000 in renovations — which you probably wouldn't have to — you could still DOUBLE YOUR MONEY!

You literally can make a fortune in foreclosures. Not only can you purchase at an unbelievably low price, you can even get money from the government for the rehab repairs! The US Department of Housing and Urban Development (HUD) has loan programs for these foreclosed properties needing a little extra care. Contact your local HUD office or visit www.hud.gov.

You know, the banks got themselves into this mess and I don't feel sorry for the bankers who have too many houses on their hands. The whole foreclosure debacle still gets me riled, but this is the time for opportunity in the housing market.

Go out and nab some found money!

CHAPTER 17

Bye Bye Debt

What happens when you get out of debt? YOU HAVE MORE MONEY!

If you know about Debt Cures, you know I am passionate about reducing or eliminating debt. The banks and the credit card companies and the government all have their hands in how you got into debt. If you need help in getting out of debt, I literally wrote the book on it.

Debt Cures They Don't Want You to Know About (www. debtcures.com) is jam packed with methods and techniques to get your debt down fast. For the purposes of this Free Money book, I will highlight a few tips to get you out of debt and get that found money back where it belongs — in your pockets!

Debt Help

The government spends millions every year in free debt counseling. I know it seems ironic, but take advantage of every free service you can and especially take advantage of free services from the government.

Your tax dollars fund this country. Anything you can utilize in return is exactly what you want to do.

Check out www.hud.gov. And while I am mentioning HUD, there is a chance that you could be entitled to a refund, if you had an FHA-insured mortgage. To find out, for free, if HUD owes you a refund, visit www.hud.gov/offices/hsg/comp/refunds/.

There are also nonprofit debt counseling services that are FREE, like GreenPath (www.greenpath.com). And just a few pages back, I listed a gazillion free legal service options. They can help you with debt, bankruptcy, foreclosure, refinancing, etc.

I am also here to offer free debt advice.

Cure Your Debt

The truth is, there is only one person you need to reduce or eliminate your debt, and that person is you. I am going to give you some tasks or assignments. If you do them, your debt can go bye bye. And that means hello cash for you.

Okay, here we go. Get out your credit cards. Any card that you carry a balance on, call them. Ask for a lower interest rate. It's that simple. Follow my lead:

"Hello, my name is Kevin Trudeau and I have been an account holder with you for many years. I see that my interest rate is now up to 15% and that is simply too high. I need a much lower rate. What is the best you can do for me?"

Just like dealing with a used car dealer, let them throw out the first number.

"Well, Mr. Trudeau, I can reduce that rate to 11%."

They may or may not deal with you. You may have to ask to speak to the supervisor or manager.

"Hmmm. 11%. I can get a better deal with XXX credit card offer that came in the mail today. If you can't meet or beat their rate, I will close my account with you and transfer my balance."

"Let's see, how does 0% for six months sound and then 5% after that?"

"Sounds great, thank you."

Don't laugh, reader. Deals like that happen every day. This simple tactic works and it can save you hundreds or thousands of dollars. Reducing your interest reduces your payment and your overall balance due.

> Reducing your interest reduces your payment and your overall balance due.

It is money that you are NOT paying them, and paying to yourself. Ch-ching. More found money.

Reduce Fees

The same goes for all those fees, fees, fees, that the banks and credit card companies charge. I hate fees but we won't get into that. You can get rid of fees and pocket the money instead.

Yes, you can get rid of fees.

It takes one tool, the telephone, and one weapon, you. If you got hit with a late fee or an over-the-limit fee or any kind of crazy fee that they throw at you, call them up. Call the bank or the credit card company and ask them to remove the fee.

Just like in the example above, be polite but be firm and consistent. Ask and you shall receive. And if not, "demand," ever so politely, that the fees be taken off your account.

I have a friend who discovered that was the magic word. He was talking to the customer service representative at his credit card company, asking for the fee to be wiped off his account. Most of the time asking works, but this CSR paused and asked: "Sir, are you demanding that the fees be removed?"

His intuition kicked in, and he replied, "Yes, I am. I demand it."

And guess what? This is what he was told: "Well, all right then, I will remove the fees from your account."

He is under the impression that the "rule book" at this particular company instructed customer service representatives to say no if the customer merely asked for fees to be waived, but if the customer demanded, then don't lose the customer.

It is like the old adage, the squeaky wheel gets the grease. The squeaky wheel gets the fees removed.

Stand Your Ground

> Rule number one is to review your statements every month.

The key is to not be intimidated. They will slap fees on you willy-nilly if you let them. Times are tough, and the banks and the credit card companies are trying to beef up their revenues by sticking it to you every way they can. Credit card interest rates are being jacked up with no reason or warning. Credit limits are being reduced, again with no notice or justification, so they can hit you up with an over the limit fee.

Rule number one is to review your statements every month. Rule number two is to call right away to get rid of fees and high interest rates. Rule number three is to negotiate the actual principle balance.

As I have said, these are drastic economic times. The reality is that this is also the time for negotiation. You can haggle on fee and interest rates, and you can reduce the balance that you owe.

Let's take Sally. Sally lost her job and is working part-time at a diner. She owes $3,000 on her credit card. The minimum monthly payment is too steep and the balance is only that high because every month, the interest piles up because she can't pay it off.

Sally made the call to reduce her interest rate and it never occurred to her to ask to reduce the principle or cut a deal. Then the light bulb went on.

Sally: "I have been laid off from my job for months now and my credit card balance keeps going up even though I am no longer charging on it. Because I paid less than the minimum payment, the fees and interest were more than the amount I paid. The bill is higher the next month even after I make a payment. It is nuts."

Sound like anyone you know?

Sally had to get off this merry-go-round that was becoming more like an avalanche. She called her credit card company and got the minimum payment reduced and the fees waived and the interest rate lowered. All well and good, but she still had a large balance and no real job in order to pay it off.

Sally called the credit card company again.

"I have a balance of $3,000 and with my loss of work, I simply cannot pay it. The funds just aren't there. What I propose is that you remove from that balance all the accumulated past interest and fees. If we can get down to just the original purchases I made, I will be able to manage to pay it off."

The reply? "Okay."

It Works

Maybe it didn't happen quite that fast or quite that direct, but Sally was able to negotiate down to where she could pay. That amount that she did not pay? FOUND MONEY! She has those funds to use elsewhere now.

There are many techniques to use to get rid of debt. This kind of negotiation can be applied to car loans, personal loans, etc.

Because times are so tough, there are a lot of unscrupulous scoundrels out there trying to take advantage of people's fear. Let me clue you in to their ways so you know what tactics to use to ward them off.

Who are the scoundrels? The bill collectors. Not the usual collection agency guys; they're bad enough. There is another breed on the loose that will do practically anything to get a buck out of you.

What these guys (and gals) do is buy up old accounts from credit card companies or collection agencies and they go after this old debt. They want you to think that they have the right to collect and that you have to pay them. Don't fall for it!

Collectors

The first piece of advice I need to give you when it comes to debt collectors, any debt collectors, is never give them any information and do not acknowledge the debt as yours. There is so much mix-up and mess in the financial world, you could very well get a collection call on a debt that is not yours.

If contacted by a collection agency, always refer to the debt as the "alleged debt." Use sentences like: "I have no knowledge of that alleged debt." "That alleged debt does not appear to be in my records." "You will have to provide me documentation of that alleged debt."

Never admit that it is yours. Make them give you information in writing. Sometimes that is enough for them to back off. These goons want to deal with the people who are afraid of them because they think they can get more money that way.

What these thugs are doing is plain old fashioned bullying. They are trying to get your milk money. Don't give it up.

Old Debt

The worst thing is when they call up people for old debt. The collector dudes buy this old debt for pennies on the dollar. The holder of the debt, the credit card company, long ago wrote off the account. The collector bulldogs do not have much invested so any amount they collect is profit.

But the debt is uncollectible. They are going after money that there is no legal obligation for you to pay! They are banking on the fact that you won't know that, though.

Let's run through an example. You get a phone call from Buster Blowhard, who tries to put the squeeze on you for some debt that goes back a few years. You first do the pat answer about not knowing anything about the alleged debt.

If Buster proceeds to pester you, get the scoop on the alleged debt. Make Buster provide the detailed information. Then you can bust Buster's chops with the golden words "statute of limitations."

Yes, debt has a statute of limitations. In many states it is three years. Buster is trying to get payment on accounts that have expired. Sadly, many people don't realize this and they panic if a collector calls them. Collectors can be shrewd and rude. They are not going to say, "Gee, I bought up all those old debts dirt cheap and I am hoping to make a quick buck off of folks who I can intimidate."

But you are wise. You know to fight their scare tactics with the facts. The next phone call from Buster, all you have to say is: "The statute of limitations on this alleged debt is expired. Goodbye."

End of story. It is amazing that debt, no matter how large, can be eliminated with the statute of limitations. The statute period varies from state to state. Look up your state in the table provided in Appendix II.

And another heads up: Sometimes these greedy collection geeks will try to collect on debt that they know is not yours and/or debt that you have already paid! Can you imagine paying twice?!

So use your common sense and use the golden words.

CHAPTER 18

Your House

Yes, your house is a source of free money! There are several techniques that can allow your home to put money in your pocket.

Some people think that a home equity line is what I am talking about. I have nothing against home equity loans or home equity lines of credit. That can be a great way to get quick liquid cash.

If you go that route, just remember that the amount has to be paid back at some point, so make sure you get the best interest rate possible.

There are other ways that your house can be your haven and a nest of money, too. How about reducing your house payment? Every month you spend x amount of dollars on the mortgage. What if you paid less every month? Wouldn't that be exciting?!

Extra money to pay off other bills. Extra money to put to kids' education. Extra money to take a vacation. The list of possibilities goes on and on.

There are ways to reduce that house payment. One way — refinance. Get a better rate and get a lower payment.

Loan Modification

> It's an adjustment to your loan to lower your payment.

But maybe right now, that is not the best option. The mortgage mess has the banks twisted in knots. Maybe what you need is a loan modification.

What is that?

It's an adjustment to your loan to lower your payment. Sometimes a loan modification is temporary and sometimes it's not. Your lender might change terms for a few years, or for the remainder of the life of your loan. The idea is to get you into a mortgage payment that you can afford to make every month so you do not go into default and get tangled up in any possible foreclosure mess.

There are different ways to go about loan modification. Obviously, the first step is to talk to your lender. Some loans will be given a new modified lower rate, for example from 8% down to 6%, for a limited time frame, perhaps the next five years. That reduction in interest rate makes a reduction in your payment.

Some loans may get spread out over a longer time period. Instead of a 30-year mortgage, lenders are doing 40-year loan terms now. A 40-year loan at 5% is a nicely reduced lower payment, and free money in your bank account every month.

Lenders are more willing to work with you on modifying your existing mortgage these days because of all the foreclosures. They don't want any more foreclosures. They are not making money on them so they don't want them.

Hundreds of Thousands are Affected

According to CNN, in February 2009 alone, nearly 250,000 homeowners received a mortgage modification or repayment plan from their lender.

In case you are wondering about the difference between refinance and modification: refinance is paying off the old loan by opening a brand new loan. It requires a new closing and paperwork, etc., which means closing fees and title fees and all that other garbage that they charge for. A loan modification is simply making changes to your current existing loan to make it more manageable.

That same CNNMoney.com story reported that "the mortgage lending industry is responding to the needs of its customers and offering solutions that are appropriate to the current market and economic conditions," said Hope Now's director Faith Schwartz. Hope Now is the coalition of lenders, investors, and community advocacy groups who have joined together "to combat the foreclosure plague." (Source: money.cnn.com/2009/03/30/real_estate/February_Hope_Now/index.htm?postversion=2009033013)

If ever the market was ripe for mortgage loan modification, for better or worse, now is that time. The economy is still struggling. People are still fearing for their jobs. (You need to have employment in order to get the loan modified in most cases.) The impact of the government's efforts to prevent foreclosures is still too soon to tell.

Loan modification appears to be the winning program these days. When the mortgage meltdown first started rearing its ugly head, loan modifications were being done, but the bankers were still in denial over the extent of the damage they had created.

Their idea of loan modification was to simply allow missed payments to be added on to the mortgage. They, of course, would charge a penalty too, so the net result to the homeowner was more payment!

Duh. If a person can't make their house payment, making the payment even higher by adding on a fee is not going to help the situation. Hello! Any common sense out there in the finance industry??

Crisis Mode

Now that the crisis has indeed become a crisis, the banks are making loan modifications that actually do modify the monthly payment. Bravo. Follow the thought process. A person cannot make his house payment. Modify the loan in order to get a lower payment. He then can make his payment and not go into default. The foreclosure process will not be necessary and the banks can still collect some dough, and the homeowner can stay in his house. Both parties are satisfied.

It took the dense banking industry of our country a little bit of time to figure that out. They were still in greed mode. As I said, the first loan modifications were nothing more than an extension of the loan. With a penalty for the pleasure of doing so.

According to CNN, about half of the first loan modifications that were made actually resulted in a larger payment for the mort-gage holder. Things that make you scratch your head and wonder if anyone in the financial world can apply some logic. (Source: money.cnn.com/2009/04/03/news/economy/loan_modifications/index.htm?postversion=2009040313) These people were struggling to begin with and even with a so-called loan modification, they still ended up in mortgage default because they could not make their payments.

Because of the crash of the economy and the onslaught of fore-closures, loan modifications are now living up to their name. They are actually getting modified, not just an "Oh yeah, we'll give you a couple more months to pay."

The government's housing plan gives money to the banks to subsidize the banks giving a lower interest rate to you. Yeah, I hear what you're thinking: Too bad the new administration did not give the money directly to the homeowners.

Forbearance

There is also something else called forbearance. If you are having trouble making your payments, you may be able to get a forbearance, which is a temporary suspension of your payments for a few months. Hopefully in that few months, you will get back on track and be able to make regular monthly payments again.

> A temporary suspension of your payments for a few months.

As long as you have a job, the odds for modifying your loan are in your favor. The federal government passed a new bill in March 2009 for the hurting homeowners. The Making Home Affordable Program, according to the *LA Times*, "provides $75 billion in financial incentives to lenders so that they will reduce interest payments.

In some cases the program allows for a reduction in principal so that the monthly payment will not exceed 31% of the borrower's income, but that reduction is only temporary. The set-aside por-tion of the principal will have to be repaid when the loan is paid off or refinanced or the house is sold. "It's for homeowners who 'have experienced a significant change in income or expenses to the point that the current mortgage payment is no longer affordable,' according to program guidelines." (Source: www.latimes.com/business/la-fi-cover22-2009mar22,0,7096135.story?page=2)

Free HUD Services

> New terms for your mortgage loan means new money for you.

If you think you want to modify your loan, first talk to a mortgage counselor at your local HUD office. Their services are FREE. Find the local office at www.hud.gov. The counselor will review your income and your current mortgage and be able to determine if you are a candidate for a loan modification.

Then, make an appointment with your lender. New terms for your mortgage loan means new money for you.

A word of caution must be given here. Because things are the way they are, a lot of people are scared of losing their homes. And when there is fear, there are predators out there willing to take advantage of that fear.

You do not need to pay anyone to renegotiate your mortgage loan for you. A whole new industry has popped up. These guys are charging big bucks to talk to your bank for you. You do not need anyone to talk for you! You sure as heck don't need to pay thousands of dollars for this "service."

Yeah, the fee can get quite ridiculous. Please note that there are legitimate nonprofit organizations out there that will help with your loan renegotiation, and they may charge a very small fee. The ones that charge three to five grand are not nonprofit agencies. They are definitely trying to make a profit — off of you.

To find a nonprofit agency in your area, contact your local HUD office. To find a HUD office, go to www.hud.gov.

Give yourself $5000 free money and do it yourself!

Buyer Beware

There are no federal laws regulating this new field, so it is buyer beware. Don't waste your precious money and your precious time with the loan modification services. You can pick up the phone just as well as they can.

Many states are getting complaints from people who turned over big bucks and nothing happened. The banks started the foreclosure process and now the person had less money and less time to fight the proceedings.

If you feel a little intimidated about the whole loan process, talk to you local HUD office. Check your phone book or www.hud.gov to find the nearest office. HUD has over 2,300 nonprofit agencies nationwide that specialize in housing counseling.

Three "Magic Words"

While I am on the subject of mortgages and fighting off foreclosures, there is a tactic you need to know about. It has been all over the news because it works. If you are in the midst of foreclosure proceedings, you can stave off the final blow with three little words: "Produce the note."

The banks are saying "pay up." You need to fire back with "show up." They need to show the legal document — your mortgage — and many times they cannot do so. Yep. The paper is the proof and if they can't provide the paper, they have no proof.

This is not typically a permanent fix, but it gives you time. The courts are swamped with foreclosure cases. Most judges prefer the quick, clean cases. If your case has a snag, it can be pushed to the bottom of the pile.

While the bank is searching for the proof of your mortgage, you are awarded time. Precious time to come up with some money to pay the delinquent house payment or to renegotiate the terms of your mortgage. Most mortgages today are not held by the bank where you took out your loan. The banks bundle up the loans into investment packages and sell them off. Your paperwork can easily go missing as it changes hands.

So when you are approached with a foreclosure notice, you simply say, "Show me the note." This tactic may very well buy you the time to save your house.

Housing Help

Maybe you are not facing foreclosure. Maybe you just want to dip into your home for some found money. With a traditional thirty-year mortgage, a homeowner ends up paying about double the purchase price of the home. That's a lot of money going to interest, or the bank's pocket, instead of yours. It is possible to pay off that 30-year mortgage in much less time! That means more money for you!

Obviously, you can pay more on the principal each month. Any extra towards the principal balance reduces the amount that the interest is calculated on. Some people pay double payments every month. Some folks throw an extra hundred in with their payment each month. Most of us, however, can only afford to make our current payment.

One trick is to take your existing mortgage payment and split it up into weekly payments. What could be easier than that! Paying bills by the week is often the best thing for people on a tight budget to do anyway.

Let's take the example of Jake. His mortgage payment of $4000 is due the first of every month. Most mortgage loans allow for prepayment, so what Jake learned to do was split the $4000 into weekly installments of $1000 each. He is allowed to prepay, and he does not want to pay late and get charged a late fee. For his payment due August 1, Jake makes weekly payments of $1000 on July 7, July 14, and July 21, and then the final payment on August 1. He has made his entire payment by August 1, so there is no late fee.

> You can shave years and years off the life of your mortgage!

It does not seem like it should make any difference at all, paying your mortgage this way, but it makes a tremendous difference. The amount of interest that you pay is greatly reduced each month because the bank or mortgage firm is getting a good portion of their payment early. You are not paying nearly as much interest, and more is going toward paying your principal. You can shave years and years off the life of your mortgage! That is THOUSANDS OF DOLLARS found!

Another quick and easy method is to make *just one* extra mortgage payment each year toward your principal. Don't think this will amount to much? Think again. By making this extra payment, you could shave as much as *three years* off of a 20-year fixed rate mortgage. That adds up to a lot of extra money in your pocket — money that the lenders don't get. That is thousands of dollars that you are saving by simply making an extra payment toward principal every twelve months! This is a simple method that will keep you *years* ahead of the game!

Pay Off That Mortgage Sooner

✔ Get a loan from a family member to pay down the principal. The interest savings will allow you to repay.

✔ If you pay points on your loan, pay them up front; don't roll them into the loan. If you're not paying them up front, you'll be stuck with a higher balance that you'll be paying interest on each month.

✔ Consider a loan from your 401(k) plan to pay down your mortgage. If you can get a lower rate than your mortgage, it's a good tactic. And you are paying yourself back.

✔ Use your home as a forced savings account. Make a higher payment each month; for example, put $500 more directly toward the principal. You build up your equity faster and decrease the interest. If you need money, instead of having it sit in a savings account, you use a home equity loan or a home equity line of credit.

Mortgage Accelerator Loan

Ever heard of a mortgage accelerator loan? These loans use special accounts to encourage borrowers to apply all extra money toward their mortgages. The savings can be huge!

If you'd like to pay off that mortgage, but you lack the discipline to do so, a mortgage accelerator loan may be a great idea for you. All you have to do is refinance your home and set up an equity line of credit. The final step is to arrange it so that your paychecks from work are directly deposited into your new credit account. It is much like your regular checking account, with one distinct advantage: the money in the account reduces the balance of the mortgage and any money not paid for bills is applied against the principal balance.

With this special loan, your principal balance is decreased, and you end up saving bundles of interest! So, in essence, the paycheck goes toward paying off the house. There are currently two companies that offer this loan in the US. For more information, you can check it out at: articles.moneycentral.msn.com/Banking/HomeFinancing/ANewWayToPayOffYourHouse.aspx.

A similar product is the Money Merge Account. Combining your checking and savings accounts with an advanced line of credit, this system exists to aid you in paying off your mortgage in one-third to one-half the regular time. There is no refinancing involved, no change in the amount of your monthly payments.

> ...aid you in paying off your mortgage in one-third to one-half the regular time.

Check out this example, which is explained in more detail on www.unitedfirstfinancial.com: You have a 30-year, $136,000 mortgage at 5.25%. If you paid each month for 30 years, you would pay $270,784 — nearly twice the cost of the home. Standard operation for many folks, and the banks are quite happy with that status quo.

The Money Merge Account program, simply by applying money to the principal all the time, can help repay the same mortgage in just over 11 years. Total repayment of $181,217 — an incredible savings of $89,566! Same mortgage, same interest rate, little or no changes in your monthly expense, but wow, what a nice sum.

Lower Your Rate

Getting that lower interest rate is the most amazing thing you can do to cut time and dollars off of your mortgage. Let's take a look at what happens with differing interest rates.

INTEREST RATE	PAYMENT	30 YEARS OF INTEREST
9.3%	$1,651	$394,362
8.5	$1,542	$355,200
7.3	$1,373	$294,247
6.1	$1,220	$239,250
5.6	$1,151	$214,518
5.5	$1,136	$208,853

Is it obvious from looking at the chart? If you have 5.5% interest rate, your monthly payment is $1,136. Over thirty years, you would pay a total of $208,853 in interest. If you have an interest rate of 8.5%, your monthly payment is now $1,542. That means every month, you pay over $400 more, and that totals almost five grand in a year!

And what really hits home — over the life of the loan, you would pay out $146,347 extra! Think of what that money could be used for or invested! That is almost $150,000. The mortgage amount of this example used to run the numbers is a $200,000 mortgage. You could have bought another house!

See how much money is out there for you when you have new eyes?

PMI

Another way to put money back in your pocket is to get rid of PMI, private mortgage insurance. If you did not put 20% down on your house, the bank will charge you PMI, just another way to squeeze money out of you.

Apply all the ways to make quick cash and put money toward your equity to get you up to 20%. Borrow from friends, family, and friends of family. PMI is literally throwing money away each month.

You can also get your home reappraised to see if the change in value means your equity is now up to 20%. Simply call your mortgage company and request that your home be reappraised as it is undervalued. If your lender will not cooperate, another lender will!

The bank is supposed to automatically stop taking PMI when you have reached 22% equity in your house. It does not mean that they will. You need to pay attention and give them a call. For a mortgage balance of $200,000, you could pay over $1,000 a year in PMI! Make the call and get $1,000 in found money!

Refinance

The best way to show the dollars to you is through an easily imagined scenario. Let's take Ed and Sue. They bought their home five years ago for $300,000, with a variable rate mortgage. Their original monthly mortgage payment was $2,500. Now that five years have rolled by, interest rates have gone up as well as their principal. They are now paying $3,100 per month, and the balance is $315,000.

Ed and Sue are able to keep paying the $3,100, the amount of the monthly payment they are currently paying now. However, they should shop around and refinance the mortgage to a fixed rate. The rate they have now is astronomical. The lower rate at the beginning of the mortgage is long gone and they are now paying as high as 12%. Ed and Sue can find a fixed rate mortgage for 6 % or 7%. As we have seen, that will make a remarkable reduction in the amount of interest being paid.

By losing the old variable rate loan and switching to a new fixed rate loan, their principal will not go up, their balance will not go up, and their monthly payments will not go up. Their peace of mind will go up. They will continue to make the same monthly payment as always and now they will pay off their home much, much faster.

If you have a variable rate mortgage, what is your rate?

What should you do? Refinance!

Another way to bring the payment down, for a first-time mortgage or a refinance, is to put as much as possible in for the down payment. I understand that is a hard thing to do, so this is a prime opportunity to ask your family for help. Any money that they can loan you will save you a ton of interest! The larger your down payment, obviously the less you have to borrow, plus you qualify for a better interest rate.

Saving on interest is like saving money over and over again; better in your wallet than theirs.

CHAPTER 19

Class Action Suits

Class action suits are FREE MONEY!

You must have received a notice in the mail at one point or another, and read that you were entitled to a settlement from a class action lawsuit. What did you do with it? I know many people who throw the letter away!

That is throwing away cash.

Many Many Many

There are many, many, many open settlements ongoing, all the time. What is a class action lawsuit? In very simple terms, you are among a class of people entitled to a portion of money that is received because a company did you wrong in some way.

Maybe a telephone company mischarged for years. A class action lawsuit can be brought against the telephone company. That means not one person is suing, but the suit is filed on behalf of all it affects. Everyone who paid their bills during that time frame of the overcharges is entitled to a refund of these charges in the class action suit.

In fairly recent memory, there was a suit filed against Wal-Mart on behalf of its employees and it became the largest class action suit in history.

> ## What have you got to lose?

When you get the letter in the mail that says you are part of a class action suit, do not toss it in the trash. There usually is a short form to fill out and return. Do it. What have you got to lose?

The settlement portion that comes your way could be a few bucks, or it could surprise you.

Are You Entitled?

In addition to the suits where you are notified, you can actively search class action suits that might pertain to you. Visit www.top-classactions.com. This site is a database of the suits going on and who is entitled to receive funds.

It is amazing how many apply to the everyday, average consumer. That means you! For example, were you a Sprint Nextel customer? There is a suit with a currently open settlement for early termination fees. Get it and get your money, if this applies to you.

Maybe you are or were a Bank of America customer. The suit with BofA involved overdraft fees and over limit fees that they now have to refund. (Can I get an "Amen"?!)

This topclassactions.com website continually monitors the suits and posts the open settlements and the deadline for claiming your free money. Some settlements are forty bucks, some hundreds, some even one thousand plus. It all piles up. This Free Money is yours — claim it and take it!

You can sign up at the site to receive info, or just check in regularly to verify what may or may not apply to you. Scott, the owner of the site, collects checks every month. It is his goal for you to do the same.

You know the Lotto has a slogan that you have to play to win. For class action suits, you have to file your claim to collect. It is absolutely simple. Follow the instructions on the web, or in the mail, if you received something via our US Post Office.

It's All in the Follow-Through

Not many people follow through with the class action, and they are missing out. There was a class action suit against Ross Stores not too terribly long ago. Five thousand people filed claims. Nearly ONE MILLION people were eligible and did not file a claim! Only five thousand out of a million. If you were in that one million, don't you wish you would have received your check for nearly $250? I know I'd want my check!

It's a free website. Give a couple minutes and start watching for those checks in your mailbox. As I type, there are settlements waiting for the rightful owners to claim their cash. A Bank of America claim can net you $78; the Nextel deal is worth up to $90 to you; and $1,000 regarding Nationwide Insurance.

You can peruse the site to see what applies to you. If you ever get the opportunity to be the lead plaintiff (or the key plaintiff or a named plaintiff), that means more money for you. The court sees it as you being one of the first to bring the suit and assume you are busy with the lawyers. That means you get paid bigger bucks and you get paid first. These kinds of cases usually range from $1,000 to $10,000 for the primary people named.

Unlimited

Not a bad gig. You can collect on an unlimited number of suits. Maybe your utility company owes you something, your bank, and the company that produces your makeup. The suit could be anything.

For example, let's say you used Brand X mascara and it made your eyelashes fall out. You were not the only one. A class action suit was filed by the thousands of women who lost their eyelashes.

You could be a key plaintiff and get the big bucks. Even if you don't get in as a lead plaintiff, you still can collect free money. Collecting from all the suits that apply to you can be a nice chunk of change. A check a month is not an unrealistic goal.

The federal government has a website as well that you can use to check on the status of class action suits and the settlement dates. See www.sec.gov/divisions/enforce/claims.htm for more information.

You can review the lengthy list of companies that have class action activity to see if it affects you in any way. If so, file your claim!

Get that FREE MONEY!

CHAPTER 20

Free Money While You're Waiting on Money

We'll get into grants and all the government money that is sitting there just waiting for you in a minute or two. Let's say you want money right now, or you have applied for a grant and you are waiting for the check to come.

Here are a few quick and easy ways to get cash NOW.

$10K in a day

✔ **Referral fees/Assignment of Contract.** Want to make a large sum of cash in an amazingly short amount of time? And want to do so with no risk? I thought you might be interested. Well, there is a slight risk involved. One dollar. Willing to lose a buck? The opportunity to make huge dollars is worth that dollar investment!

An ideal way to turn a quick deal and make thousands of dollars, this strategy is certainly one of my favorites. An assignment of a contract is the key to untold cash in your coffers. The possibilities are endless and the sky is the limit when it comes to how much you can make.

Maybe you see yourself as the middleman in this scenario. I see it as the moneyman. Or woman, of course. Basically, an assignment of contract is a transaction between a person who has something to sell and you, except that you do not want the asset that the person is selling. You want money.

So you make a deal with the seller. You agree to enter into a contract to purchase the thing that he is selling. You put up $1.00 in order to make the contract legally binding and you agree to buy the asset for a certain price in a certain period of time, and here is the important part, you have an assignment clause in the contract. That means you can assign to someone else your right to buy this asset. You don't want it, whatever the "it" is; you want to make some cash on the deal. Basically, you tie up the asset for one dollar, and have the "option" to pay the balance at a given time in the future (e.g. within 30, 60 or 90 days). In essence they become the buyer and you are simply a middleman.

You have a buyer who wants the asset, or you find one. You assign the contract to this person for a price greater than your contract with the seller and you keep the difference. Snap your fingers and cash appears.

How about an example:

Bob has a house that has a value of $100,000 that he needs to sell. You contract with Bob for $1 that you will buy the house for $60,000 and your agreement states that you can assign the contract to someone else. You agree that you (or your assignee) will buy the house within 60 days or you forfeit your dollar. You then assign the contract to a buyer that you found who is willing to buy the house for $90,000. You get to keep the difference. $30,000! That is a nice return on a one-dollar investment!

Someone recently did this exact method and made over $18,000. The person tied up a piece of real estate in Phoenix, and quickly advertised it in San Francisco. He was able to assign his contract to purchase the Phoenix property to someone who responded to the advertisement and he pocketed that $18,000 plus, with zero risk!

This method can be done with real estate, cars, jewelry, furniture, artwork, etc., etc., etc. The possibilities are endless!! Just tie it up for $1 and assign that asset away!

✔ **eBay.** eBay is the way, baby! One way, anyway. I don't get any kickbacks or love money or anything for talking about eBay. It is simply hands-down an easy and sure-fire quick way to put some greenback in your wallet.

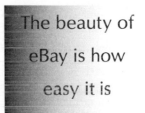

The beauty of eBay is how easy it is

I could write a book on how to use eBay, but I imagine there are already books out there that serve that purpose. eBay is hugely popular because it works. You've got something to sell and there is somebody out there that wants to buy it.

Take a look around your house. Go through the garage. Spend an hour in the attic. What has been sitting in your basement for years that you forgot you even had? If you are a "normal" American, you hang on to stuff for the eternal "just in case I might need it someday." We end up with a lot of stuff that we never use. I know a guy who keeps everything, but then when he does need it, he can't find it. So he goes out and buys another one. He has two sets of painting supplies, two of a lot of tools, you get the idea.

Even if you are not a stockpiler or hoarder or an unorganized "where did I put that?" kind of person like my friend, I can pretty much guarantee that you have stuff you can get rid of. We all do. If you can see that your stuff really is cash in your pocket, it makes it easier to part with.

Got golf clubs that you haven't used in three years? Get rid of them. Maybe a bike or roller blades? If you have kids, you have a never-ending turnover of stuff that you can get rid of when they outgrow it or tire of it. Famous brand children's clothing makes a killing on eBay. Their toys, your toys, your tools, the possibilities are endless.

The beauty of eBay is how easy it is and how easy it is for you to get paid. Set up a PayPal account (it's quick and easy and requires no technical savvy), and the payments you receive are deposited right into your PayPal account. You don't have to deal with credit cards or worrying if the buyer's check is going to bounce. You just sit back and watch the balance in your account go up, up, up.

You could make $10K in a day just from eBay. But there are nine more ways to make fast money. Actually there are many more, but 10 ways to $10K in a day has such a great ring to it.

✔ **craigslist.** The other great Internet gold mine besides eBay is craigslist. There really is a guy named Craig who started an online version of a buy it/sell it bulletin board. Remember in college when people would post little notes by the campus mailbox? "Need a ride to San Diego this weekend." "Have a motorcycle to sell." "Looking for a roommate this summer?"

The concept is the same, but the venue has gone global. If you have something to offer, there is someone looking for it and they will look on craigslist. Go to www.craigslist.com and check it out. The possibilities are endless.

Sell your car, motorcycle, scooter, boat, Winnebago RV, your electronics, your jewelry, your collectibles. If you have a vacation home, rent it for a week and make big bucks fast.

If you live in New York or any other cool place that people want to visit, rent out your apartment for a week and get quick cash. It is amazing the transactions that can happen if you use your creative mind. Think cash and think fast and it will be yours.

✔ **Sell your car.** You can use eBay or craigslist or any other online site. You can set it in front of your house with a For Sale sign. You can run an ad in your local paper. You can take it to a used car lot and see what they will give you. You can simply tell a friend to tell everyone he knows that you have a car for sale.

Word of mouth is often the best way to get things done and costs you nothing. If you live in a metropolitan area with good public transportation, you honestly do not need a car. I know of a gal who lives in Chicago about a block from the train station. She walks to everything in her local neighborhood and when she needs a car, there is a car rental place just a few blocks away. She can walk there and rent a car for only as long as she needs, even just for an afternoon.

The money she spends to rent a car on occasion is much less than the cost of car payments, insurance, and maintenance. And parking. If you have lived in a city, you know what a hassle parking can be.

Maybe you simply can't live without your car. Or you think you can't anyway. I suggest letting the idea gel for a while. Motor scooters are a great alternative transportation. And when you need to take a long road trip, borrow a buddy's wheels. Or call the rental guys.

If you have a boat, you can sell it and have a large chunk of change immediately. Are you an avid boater? If not, think about how much you spend on the watercraft and how much enjoyment you get out of it. If you are in a climate where you only have three months of boating weather and you are paying for storage the other nine months, selling your boat can be an instant cure and instant fast cash. Again you can use all the ways mentioned above to sell it that don't cost you one red cent and the net gain can be tremendous.

✔ **Sell your collections.** Most folks have something that they have been hanging on to for years and then they reach a point in their lives when their interests change, and those collections no longer mean anything to them. Are you a collector? Then there is cash to be had.

> You can buy and sell and make a nice sum.

The baseball cards you have been collecting since you were a kid have value. If the sentimental value is no longer there for you, it's time to cash in. There are other collectors out there that want your stash, and there are buyers simply because there is money there. If you are knowledgeable, you can buy and sell and make a nice sum. You can sell off or you can be a trader.

I know of a guy who is a collector of old and rare coins. He makes great money selling to stores and other collectors. There are all kinds of collectibles out there. Stamps, postcards, antique toys, trinkets, and glassware from different eras. If your passion is Depression glass or Victorian silver, there is a market.

Maybe you are not a collector now. If this area interests you as a way to make fast money, you can get up to speed on the value and availability of certain collectibles by researching the Internet and magazines and other publications on that particular item and area of interest.

People make great money at flea markets and antique shows and estate sales. If you know about potbelly stoves or beaded jewelry or what have you, the money is there to be made. And you can have a lot of fun in the process.

✔ **Event Tickets.** Maybe instead of stuff, you are into events. Concerts, sporting events, fighting matches, theatre, dance, etc, etc. The show must go on and somebody always needs a ticket. You can be the go-to guy.

I am not telling you to be a ticket scalper. I am suggesting that there is money to be made as a ticket reseller. It is legal most places. Don't get into trouble if it's not legal in your town!

Think of quick, easy cash. You buy tickets for the rock show coming to town and word gets out that you have the hot seats. You can advertise or you can let your friends do the vocal PR for you. Your phone will be ringing and ch-ching, you will be collecting green with no effort.

There are also lots of online opportunities to resell tickets. Some sites like StubHub are for buying and selling. Use your creativity and you will be making lots of cash in very little time.

✔ **Take a loan against your 401(k).** If you have a nice nest egg in the retirement account and want money right here, right now, tap into the money sitting there. You get it quick, you get a good interest rate, and you are paying yourself back, not a bank.

✔ **Take a loan against other investment accounts.** Same logic applies here as well. Quick liquid cash available when you need it. Pay back yourself at a good rate.

✔ **Cash advance on your credit card.** If you need money now, take advantage of the credit card in your wallet. You can get immediate cash in the blink of an eye.

✔ **Phone a friend.** Maybe you have a friend or relative who owes you money. Now is the time to collect. Or maybe you have a friend or relative who always offers you a loan. If you want quick cash in a jiffy, accept the loan with a heartfelt thanks. Maybe they will even give it to you interest free.

✔ **Get an advance from your employer.** Depending upon your type of work and method of payment, you may be able to get an advance from your employer. If you know you have a good commission check coming next month, take it as an advance now, if you need the funds pronto.

✔ **Equity line.** If you are a homeowner, access your home equity line of credit. You can get big sums, pay little interest, and have the cash in hand in the snap of a finger.

✔ **Consult.** Find consulting jobs that pay an advance. You can use your expertise to make a quick buck. People need what you know. You need fast cash. Find a consulting job by word of mouth or online at www.csc.com, www.careerbuilder.com, and http://ops-jobs.theladders.com/Management-Consulting.

✔ **Licensing.** License your product or idea to an infomercial company. Infomercial companies are often willing to see you on short notice and move aggressively, if they like your product. Many are willing to pay $10–30,000 just for licensing plus a royalty. That is FAT cash FAST!

✔ **Audition.** Audition for modeling opportunities. No, not "those kind" of gigs. There are legitimate needs for print and video ads. Television commercials need local people. Maybe you can audition for acting parts as well.

✔ **Your house.** Live in a town where things happen? Super Bowl, Final Four, Olympics? Rent out your house during that week. People will pay huge money!

✔ **Think timely.** While I am on the subject of big events, sell time sensitive items when the time is hot and you can make outrageous sums of money. Sell Super Bowl champion shirts the week of the big game. Sell the big concert shirts. Use that brain and your purse will thank you.

✔ **Get a loan.** That seems like a no-brainer so we overlook the obvious. Need money fast? Get a loan from a local guy or check out the online lenders. See www.pacificadvance.com or www.bankfreedom.com/learnmore.html.

✔ **Go for the gold.** When I talk about there being a gold mine of opportunities out there for you to get quick cash, I mean it. People are having gold parties these days at their homes. Turn in your old outdated gold jewelry (or from the last marriage) and get big money that night. You may be glad you dumped him when you see how much the loot brings you. Visit www.cash4gold.com.

I originally thought I had "10 ways to $10K," but that list I just rattled off is way more than ten ways. And once you start thinking, you will come up with even more. There is no end to how you can get money when you need it.

Government Bucks

Even the government can help. Yep. Let's say you have been accepted for SSI — Social Security Income payments. If you live in Rhode Island, they have a bridge fund to tide you over while you are waiting. $200 a month is a nice bridge. For details on this particular program, see www.dhs.state.ri.us/dhs/adults/dgpadult.htm.

If you are saying, "But Kevin, I don't live in Rhode Island," I hear you. The point is that programs are all over, everywhere, here and there, and may be in your state, too. For example, Minnesota has general assistance monthly cash payments — for details and information see http://www.co.anoka.mn.us/v1_departments/div-human-services/dept-income-maintenance/cash-programs.asp.

Kansas — $350 per month — www.srskansas.org/ISD/ees/ga.htm to see if you qualify.

California — varies per county — www.dss.cahwnet.gov/cdss-web/PG132.htm for more info and details.

> There is no end to how you can get money when you need it.

Are you catching the wave? There is money out there, for you.

Of course, using more than just one of the aforementioned techniques gives you the greatest chance of success. Any one of the tactics listed above can get you there, but those timeless words of wisdom ring true here: don't put all your eggs in one basket.

To make sure you hit your target, you throw more than one dart, so try more than one of these suggestions. You never know which will be most successful for you.

Seek and you shall find! $10K in a day! Let me know your success stories!

Chapter 21

Grants

For some of you, you may have flipped right here to the start of grants. I hope not. Honestly, grants are great — beyond great — but so are the free/found money ideas that we covered in the first twenty chapters.

So if this is the first chapter you are reading, go back and crack open the book at the beginning. I don't want you to miss out on anything!

Greenback From the Red, White and Blue

For the rest of you who have been with me all the way, I do admit that I get excited about government grants. Money from Uncle Sam that you never have to repay! That is FREE MONEY in all its glory!

There are grants for EVERYTHING!

Personal needs, business needs, go to school, start a small business, fix up your house, travel abroad, the list is endless!

One of the remarkable things with grants (besides the fact that it is money given to you that you never have to pay back) is that grants are not based on credit scores or credit history or any of that kind of credit mumbo-jumbo that makes people nervous.

A lot of people have bad credit. It doesn't mean a thing to the grant people. Credit scores try to measure your ability to repay a loan. Grants are not loans, so the grant givers don't care if you are able to repay because the money is yours to keep!

So if you are worried about your credit score (read *Debt Cures* for all the help you need), worry no more. Grant applications do not ask about your credit.

Another wonderful thing about grants is that you don't have to stop at one. You can apply for as many grants as you want!

Income Not The Issue With Grants

And I know that some of you are thinking that you have to be "poor" in order to qualify for a grant. Not true! There are many grants that have no consideration at all for income level! Lots of the rich and famous have received grants. Even George W. Bush, before he was president, received grant money for his baseball team's new stadium.

> You can apply for as many grants as you want!

Government grants come from federal, state, and local branches. Private grants come from companies and foundations. And because many people don't know about these grants, or they assume that they would not qualify, a lot of this money is going unclaimed.

As I explained earlier in this book, when bills are passed in Congress, the boys in Washington throw in a little something for their pet projects, like education, women business owners, farmers, etc. That is how money from the government gets set aside for grants. It is there and cannot be repurposed somewhere else.

Private foundations have to give away so much in funding to keep their nonprofit status and tax-exempt status. They are set up as a foundation and have to give away a certain percentage of their assets. Foundations can determine any cause for their grants. That is why there are so many different — and unique — opportunities.

If you are a banjo-playing scientist looking for a grant to study the mating habits of caterpillars, there very well could be a grant out there for you. Obviously, I made that up, but you get my point. Private foundations can give money to whomever and for whatever they see as a cause fitting their mission.

Be it government or private, there is money sitting there waiting for you! Tell everyone you know and go for it!

Nothing Out of Pocket

With grants, there is no up-front money for you to dish out. You fill out an application — we will get to the nitty gritty in a jiffy — and they let you know if you will be awarded a grant. There is no processing fee or application fee, so you have nothing to lose.

Maybe you are a little familiar with grants, but have been too overwhelmed by the sheer magnitude. I understand. It would be great if there was one big clearing house for all the grants available and all you had to do was submit one application. A magic elf would sift through all the possibilities and let you know all you qualified for.

It does not work that way in real life. There is not one government office in charge of all grants. All the individual agencies manage their own grant programs. That means you have to apply to each separate agency.

And that is where some people get overwhelmed. They don't know where to begin. I am playing the part of the magic elf and helping you get started. This is where you begin. Right here, right now.

The categories are endless. What do you want money for? Give it a Google search and see what you can find.

Buying a Home

There are hundreds of programs for home assistance, especially if you are a first time home buyer. Try this site:

> There are hundreds of programs for home assistance.

www.first-time-homebuyer-site.com/down_payment/down_payment_assistance_information.htm.

You can also find your state immediately by doing a Google search with "First Time Home Buyer Program" and the name of your state.

It can be overwhelming, all the options out there. For example:

✔ Texas offers a grant equal to 5% of the mortgage on the home.

Texas Department of Housing and Community Affairs
www.tdhca.state.tx.us/homeownership/fthb/buyer_intro.htm

✔ Texas also has tax credits (gotta love those tax credits!) for mortgages.

Texas Mortgage Credit Program
www.tdhca.state.tx.us/homeownership/fthb

✔ Kentucky has a Down Payment Assistance Program.

www.kyhousing.org/page.asp?sec=54&id=70

✔ California has a variety of programs.

California Homebuyers Downpayment Assistance
Programs (CHDAP)
www.calhfa.ca.gov/homebuyer/

✔ Minnesota has its share of programs, too.

www.first-time-home-buyer-s.com/first_time_home_buyer_
grant_minn.htm

✔ Iowa offers up to $2,500 in assistance for down payment or
closing costs.

Iowa Finance Authority
www.iowafinanceauthority.gov/en/for_home_buyers/

✔ Look into the FHA (Federal Housing Authority) for
programs. (www.fha.com/fha_programs.cfm)

✔ The site www.FHA.com has links to programs such as
AmeriDream, which offers grants for down payments and
closing costs for up to 10% of the purchase price of the
home; and The Nehemiah Program, which provides down
payment assistance; and American Family Funds, which also
helps with down payments and closing costs.

The above is just a sampling. Closing costs? Can get them paid.
Need help with the down payment? Can get it paid. Repairs and
rehab? Can get funds for that, too.

Every state has mortgage programs. To search your state, give
a click on www.cc-bc.com/state_grants.html.

There are homeowner assistance programs that are not just for first-time buyers. People who need emergency help with the house payment can find aid. Google "Homeowners Emergency Assistance Programs" and the name of your state.

For example:

✔ Pennsylvania grants loans up to $60,000.

www.phfa.org/consumers/homeowners/hemap.aspx

✔ Delaware grants loans up to $15,000.

www.destatehousing.com/services/hb_demap.shtml

✔ City of Minneapolis has grants of $10,000 ($1.5 million available).

http://www.ci.minneapolis.mn.us/mayor/news/20090107newsmayor_Homebuyerprogramsgetsfunds.asp

✔ Minneapolis also offers no interest loans of $10,000.

www.ci.minneapolis.mn.us/cped/minneapolisadvantage_home.asp

✔ Many real estate firms offer information on state programs.

www.localism.com/blog/mn/posts/894486/home-buyer-programs-in

> There is a wealth of home buyer and home owner assistance programs out there!

ALL of these sites have all the details you will need to know, like any income limits, how to apply, phone numbers to call with questions, etc.

In case it is not obvious, there is a wealth of home buyer and home owner assistance programs out there! Free money waiting. Go for it!

Energy

How about a little energy boost? There are programs available in every state. Need help to pay the heating bills in winter? It's available. There are summer programs, too. If you are in need, there is free money for you.

The LIHEAP (Low Income Heating Energy Assistance Program) has links to all state programs at www.liheap.ncat.org/sp.htm. When the heating bills go up, it is nice to know there is assistance for those who need it.

For example, in Massachusetts (http://www.liheap.ncat.org/), there is a discount of 20–40% on utility bills plus a 5% senior citizen discount. Free services are also available to make homes more energy efficient. Things like wall insulation, attic insulation, air scaling, and heating system replacement are provided by these programs.

More residential energy support programs are available through APS. See www.aps.com.

How about discounts on phone service? There are programs that offer that, too. Visit www.lifeline.gov.

Child Safety

How about free child car seats?

Different programs in different communities. Call your local United Way office, local police department, or check with your hospital and insurance company, in addition to the programs listed below. Some states have programs that "rent" car seats for five dollars.

Infant Car Seats
BabyLove
800-395-2229

KARS (Kids Are Riding Safe)
Goodwill Easter Seals Miami Valley
http://gesmv.easterseals.com/site/PageServer?pagename=
OHWC_KARS

Visit the National Highway Traffic Safety Administration
(NHTSA) — www.nhtsa.dot.gov — for info on safety seats and
how to properly secure your child.

Looking for Work

How about getting a job? Does that sound like a nice chunk of
found money? If you have been out of work for a while, it sure does.
Many people have lost their jobs these past months. Think about
your career plans. Think about education. This is a smart time to
think about becoming a teacher. Money is going to be funneled into
school programs and school building and SCHOLARSHIPS.

If you have a desire to teach, now is a wonderful opportunity.
Even if you are not exactly a traditional age student, you can go
back and get your degree. Teachers with a little life experience are
scholarship eligible, too.

Another huge need is in the field of nursing. Scholarship money
is ready and waiting for you to apply for it. A severe nurse shortage
is on the horizon. Most nurses get to pick their schedules and their
pay is great, usually full-time pay for less than full-time hours.

Just one of many money opportunities for nursing is at

www.courseadvisor.com/site/2230105?pubid=1231.

According to the U.S. Department of Labor, health care occupa-
tions are projected to create more than 3 million new job openings
between 2004 and 2014, including:

✔ Medical Assistants

✔ Health Information Technologists

✔ Medical Coding & Billing Specialists

✔ Medical Record Transcriptionists

✔ Registered Nurses (RN)…more than 600,000 needed, and the number of online nursing programs continues to rise.

You can get your nursing degree online and schedule your work hours around your family. That's a win-win!

Another program has $2 million in scholarship funds available — that's a whole lotta help for a whole lotta people. The beauty of this scholarship is what a need it fulfills. What are the hardest things for a working parent to overcome? Time and money. The scholarship provides the time and the program is online so parents can make the time to go back to school!

Working Moms

Project Working Mom grants full-ride scholarships for online degrees. How amazing is that! Having the flexibility to take courses around the schedule of work and kids is brilliant. And having it all paid for is a dream come true for the recipients of these funds.

> Project Working Mom grants full-ride scholarships for online degrees.

This organization now offers applications to men, too. For more information on Project Working Mom…and Dads Too!, visit www. projectworkingmom.com. One mom, Donna G, who went back to school said, "I didn't know how I was going to finance my second semester with the economy going the way it is."

She came across the Project Working Mom scholarship while she was online one morning. She filled out the application that day and Donna was awarded a full-ride scholarship to Penn Foster College. The program also retroactively paid for what she had spent the first semester!

Donna was interviewed by her local newspaper. "I was really, really excited I was able to get a full scholarship," she said, adding she hopes it inspires her children. "It will be positive for them to see me get my degree and, hopefully, they will follow in the same path."

(www.theadobepress.com/articles/2009/02/13/news/news03.txt)

Inspiration comes in many forms and what better way than to have a full-ride scholarship! Free money!

Volunteers

Just when I think I cannot be surprised, I learn something that surprises me. It's a pleasant surprise. You can volunteer and get paid for it.

> You can volunteer and get paid for it.

Go to www.seniorcorps.org. Some volunteers can earn an hourly tax-free stipend. You can also receive accidental and liability insurance while doing your volunteer duties. That is something to get excited about! A stipend, getting paid for what you love to do.

Look up Volunteers of America. You can get $200 per month. And paid time off and holidays! See www.voa.org.

If you are age 60 or over and want to spend time with children, this is a way to do something you love, a way to give back to a child, and get some free money. Does the role of foster grandparent appeal to you?

You can spend time with a child, change that child's life, and ultimately change yours as well.

Foster grandparents give a few hours a week to tutor a child and help with reading. You are, in essence, giving love and support, the main role of grandparents. You can do this for up to 40 hours per week and get paid.

According to seniorcorps.gov, people who volunteer live longer and have a positive outlook on life. Is that you?

For more information on volunteer programs that provide the volunteers stipends, plus meals, transportation, insurance, an annual physical exam, a uniform, if needed, and recognition activities, view the Seniorcorps website, Volunteers of America and the Resource Center at www.nationalserviceresources.org/sc-fgp-handbook or call 800-860-2684.

The state of New York has launched a special savings plan for low income New Yorkers called $aveNYC Accounts. The city will match a portion of the tax refund that the resident deposits into this account. It encourages savings and the match is FREE MONEY.

For more info, go to www.nyc.gov/consumers.

Many states offer unique programs.

Search and Find

Searching for grants can be like being a kid in a candy store. There is so much to choose from, with some amazing resources online for finding and applying for grants:

Try www.govengine.com. This site is enormous. It is the monster of government sites. So much information, it boggles the brain. Use it to guide you to all state agency information and national as well. When I say it is overwhelming it is because there is so much to sift through; I am not kidding. That is why I am telling you how to use someone else who has already done the sifting. Try www.fdncenter. org. On this site, you are able to "search four complete databases — Grant makers, Companies, Grants, and 990s — to retrieve the latest facts on over 96,000 funders and 1.5 million grants."

To search the database of nonprofit organizations in the US, try www.guidestar.com. There are close to 1.8 million nonprofits in our country. And many of those give grants and low cost loans.

There is MUCH MUCH MORE.

First, you have to check out www.govbenefits.gov. This site has information on thousands of programs. It is easy to navigate. There are two ways to maneuver this site. Let's assume you have no idea what you might qualify for or what you are looking for specifically. Click on the "Start Here" button. It will take you to an easy-to-answer questionnaire.

There are some questions to go through and depending upon how fast you read, it will take you 5 to 10 minutes to complete. The questions are simple and straightforward, and completely anonymous. You do not give your name or social security number. The only personal questions are age, gender, and income level. After you answer the questions, a list of possible grant or benefit programs pops up that you could be eligible for.

You then can review the list of agencies and programs that you have pre-qualified for based upon the answers to your questions.

This feature alone can save you days and weeks, if not months and years, of time searching for possible free money sources.

If you already know where your interest lies, for example, "utilities" or "education," you can also use the Quick Search feature on govbenefits.gov. Select the topics, which include: Awards; Counseling; Disaster Relief; Financial Assistance; Grants, Scholarships, Fellowships; Housing; Loans; Social Security/Pension; Child Care; Disability Assistance; Education; Food; Health Care; Insurance; Medicare; and Utilities. A list of all the programs in that category appears.

Click each one that interests you or that is in your state. Then you can view the details of each, or click to see if you could be eligible. You answer a few questions, and what you may be eligible for is narrowed down. Some of the free money sources are limited to your income level, but even if you have a high income, there are still low-cost loan opportunities on this site.

www.grants.gov

Another fantastic resource that is not widely known or publicized is: www.grants.gov.

Most federal agencies who offer grants post them here. You can read about the grant, see if you qualify, and download and submit your application, all online. Instead of having to search through hundreds of different agency programs, this site allows you to look for what you may be able to apply for, in one location. There are hundreds of grant programs from many agencies on this site; billions of dollars to be awarded!

> www.grants.gov. Most federal agencies who offer grants post them here.

With www.grants.gov, the search process through the maze of federal grants out there has been connected into one big site where you have to enter your information just once. You can look at grants by agency name or by category.

You can become aware of grants and sources that you would not have known about. If you just want to browse through the grants, you do not have to register. If you want to apply for a grant, you will need to register. Follow the instructions on the website. They also provide a user guide for you at: www.grants.gov/assets/ GDG_AppUserGuide_0207.pdf.

SBA

There are also many programs through the Small Business Administration that you should not overlook. These are not all grants, but loans with very good interest rates and easy terms.

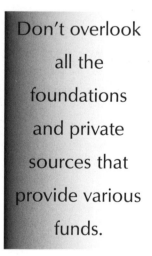

Don't overlook all the foundations and private sources that provide various funds.

Don't overlook all the foundations and private sources that provide various funds. See: www.foundationcenter.org/ getstarted/individuals/ or www.fundsne-tservices.com or www.kn.pacbell.com/ products/grants/locate.html. Thousands of possibilities are at your fingertips.

The official website of the federal government, USA.gov (www.usa.gov), contains valuable information about all US government agencies. The first topic listed is Benefits and Grants. This link gives you lots of official information on grants, loans, financial aid, and other benefits from the US government. You can even sign up to be notified when the benefits page is updated.

Govloans.gov (www.govloans.gov) is your gateway to government loan information. This site directs you to the loan information that best meets your needs and is an excellent source for locating loans for children, agriculture, business, disaster relief, education, housing, veterans, or just about anything for which you might need a loan.

The Small Business Administration has implemented programs that have drastically changed the futures of the individuals and the companies that have qualified for them.

There's the Small Business Innovation Research program, also known as the SBIR. In an effort to stimulate the forward-thinking aspects of qualifying small businesses, the SBIR offers a host of monetary awards, some totaling as much as $100,000. (www.sba.gov/SBIR/indexsbir-sttr.html)

The SBA Office of Technology also has the Small Business Technology Transfer Program (STTR). Five federal departments award $2 billion to small high-tech businesses in this program. If that is your business and you have fewer than 500 employees, you can apply to get a piece of that $2 billion pie. The Small Business Administration offers other great free money programs, and you can learn more about them here: www.sba.gov. I cannot begin to list everything, but I hope you get the idea that the money is there, and I hope you see that finding it is not as hard as you may have thought.

The List is Long

Federal money programs, grants, and loans:

✔ $25,000 "micro-loan" to start a business — www.sba.gov

✔ $200,000 to run a ranch or a farm — www.fsa.usda.gov

- ✔ $200,000 credit line for small businesses — www.sba.gov/financing/loanprog/caplines.html

- ✔ $500,000 to start a business — www.sba.gov

- ✔ $300,000 to help you get government contracts! — www.dla.mil/db

- ✔ $500,000 for females and minorities to get government contracts — osdbuweb.dot.gov

In addition to grants, there are many loans available that are quick, and guaranteed by the Small Business Administration. You fill out one page and can get $150,000. That is worth the time it takes to fill out a single sheet of paper! Find out about the Low Documentation Loan Program at: www.sba.gov/financing/lendinvest/lowdoc.html. There are Small Business Development Centers in every state as well. Contact: www.sba.gov/services.

Need some start-up money to get things going? Go to: www.sba.gov/aboutsba/sbaprograms/inv/index.html. The SBIC funding for small businesses includes $10 billion from the government and private funding of over $12 billion.

The SBIC site likes to share their success stories and reading them is very inspirational. Check out www.sba.gov/aboutsba/sbaprograms/inv/INV_SUCCESS_STORIES.html and see if you are in awe, as I was. They state it perfectly: "The most exciting potential of an SBIC investment is how it can turn one small company into a great success story."

Your company could join the ranks of big names (who once were small) like America Online, Apple Computer, Federal Express, Gymboree, Jenny Craig Inc, Staples, and many, many more. There is free money for your business. Who knows, you could be "small potatoes" today, and in the future, you could join the list that contains the likes of Outback Steakhouse, Restoration Hardware, and Costco.

There are hundreds of state agencies with money to help your business. Let's take a state like New York. Growing a business in New York can be tough — especially when it's technology-based. With all the fierce competition out there, it can be daunting for a business owner who hopes to transform the market with cutting-edge technologies. That is exactly why the Small Business Technology Investment Fund Program (SBTIF) exists.

> There are hundreds of state agencies with money to help your business.

Free Money at Work

Free money can change everything. Watch your business soar to heights you never imagined — all because of the venture capital you gained from the SBTIF. New York's economic development agency, Empire State Development, started this fund with the hope of nurturing all businesses based in technology. Read about this and other venture capital opportunities in New York here: www.nylovessmallbiz.com.

In a place like Rhode Island, Workforce Development is of great value. The Governor's Workforce Board knows just how important it is for employees of any business to possess the best skills and techniques. Great employees build great companies; it's a fact.

That is why the Governor's Workforce offers a series of grants to develop and train a team that will yield your business the best possible results. These Comprehensive Worker Training Grants can get you up to $50,000 of free money! If a stronger workforce is what your company needs, then this grant will be of tremendous benefit. Learn more about it here: www.rihric.com/awards.htm.

Women Business Owners

The entire purpose of the Small Business Association's Office of Women's Business Ownership is to help women achieve their dreams and improve their communities by providing assistance for starting a business. They provide training on how to get started and how to maintain a successful business, and they offer plenty of help along the way. Check out the SBA's website for all the details [www.sba.gov/aboutsba/sbaprograms/onlinewbc/index.html].

> The WBC provides assistance to new businesses and existing businesses looking to expand.

Among the wonderful resources for women is SBA's Women Business Centers (WBC). Available for guidance every step of the way, this SBA program provides resource centers all across the nation to help women get their businesses launched. Grants are available to these WBCs for five years, and there is even an option to renew for another five years. The program's mission is to "level the playing field." The WBC provides assistance to new businesses and existing businesses looking to expand.

For a complete list of the addresses, websites, and email contacts for each state, see: www.sba.gov/idc/groups/public/documents/sba_program_office/sba_pr_wbc_ed.pdf.

There are business grants available through the Women's Financial Fund (http://www.womensbusinessgrants.com/who. shtml).

Educators

This site — www.schoolgrants.org — which they dub as "your one stop site for PK–12 school grant opportunities," is an A+ site for educators. They offer grant writing tips and workshops focused solely on how to write successful grants in the area of education. In addition to help in writing grant applications, they provide a list of grants and where to find more information and opportunities. If education is your field, this is your site.

At www.foundations.org, someone else has done the searching for you and compiled a directory of charitable foundations. They've gathered the information; you simply click away. Select "Directories" and choose either "community foundations" or "corporate/private foundations."

A long list of people/organizations giving away free money pops up for you to peruse. You can then select from your area of interest/locale or a certain corporation. For example, I clicked on the Eddie Bauer corporation and learned all the charitable activities of that company, including providing scholarships through the Hispanic College Fund, which assists students attending schools all around the country. If you are a Hispanic college student, you've just found another source of money to apply for that you didn't know existed two minutes ago.

Simply finding what is available is more than half the battle in the search for free money. Sites like this get you on your way quicker, and it is so easy! Especially if you are looking for scholarships, check out all the community foundations in your state, county, and city. They usually have many private donors offering a wide variety of private scholarships.

Ten minutes spent searching these sites could land you $10,000 — a very wise investment of time and a wonderful investment in your future or the future of your student.

Grant Solutions

> Ten minutes spent searching these sites could land you $10,000,

Another site to add to your favorites: www.grantsolutions.gov. This is the web address for the Grants Center of Excellence (COE). It is a partnership between agencies within Health and Human Services, Department of Agriculture, the Denali Commission, and Department of Treasury. The COE states that these partner agencies distribute over $250 billion in grants each year.

The CFDA, Catalog of Federal Domestic Assistance, is also a great resource. This site gives access to a database of all federal programs that are available to state and local governments. You can search and find what you are eligible for and then contact the agency or program to apply. The site is updated biweekly as new programs are posted by federal agencies. See http://www.grant-moneyartcles.com/assstancehtl.

Another opportunity is a loan program of up to $10,000 for women in business (www.count-me-in.org). Also see: www.lib.msu.edu/harris23/grants/3women.htm; www.fundsnetservices.com/women.htm; or www.womensnet.net; plus a host of others. Another helpful resource, www.ehome-basedbusiness.com/articles, provides a list of 25 important telephone numbers for those launching a business.

Travel

Want to travel? See the world? Study abroad? There are ways and you don't have to pay! Try www.passportintime.com; www.ed.gov/programs/iegpsflasf/index.html; and http://www.nsep.gov/initiatives/ for scholarships and fellowships that provide significant funding for study abroad, in the amounts of up to $20,000 and even $30,000 for study in both the United States and abroad.

The National Security Education Programs funds Boren Fellowships, which provide grad students the opportunity to study languages and cultures that are deemed important to US national security. Students who desire a career in the federal government and wish to take coursework abroad should consider this opportunity. Fellowships are up to $30,000. Applications must be completed online. See: www.iie.org/programs/nsep/graduate/award.htm.

Have you finished your degree and want to continue? Many grants and fellowships are available. See: www.aauw.org/fga/fellowships_grants/; www.grants.gov; or look up grants in your field. Opportunities abound. For example, the National Institutes of Health offers programs for medical and dental students (grants.nih.gov/grants/index.cfm). You can also check out the Department of Education at: www.ed.gov/about/offices/list/ocfo/grants/grants.html. There are also many private funding sources out there. One such program offers fellowships and grants for education research (www.spencer.org). Private foundations are a wonderful source for dollars that you do not have to pay back.

For the federal government agency directory, you can contact: www.firstgov.gov or www.pueblo.gsa.gov/call or 1-880-FED-INFO.

CHAPTER 22

Foundations

Besides grants that come from government entities, there are many private foundations that give free money as well.

The sizes of the foundations, the amount of money they disburse, and the reasons for doing so are different. There is no one size fits all or one foundation fits all.

Giving Back

In February 2009, CNN reported a story of an unlikely hero. A young boy with a troubled past grows up and becomes a doctor. How troubled was his past? He stabbed a schoolmate (saved by a belt buckle of all things) and he went after his mother with a hammer (his brother was able to restrain him).

This boy had a terrible violent temper and yet was able to overcome it. He not only became a doctor, he practices at Johns Hopkins Children's Center as the director of pediatric neurosurgery.

Dr. Benjamin Carson has overcome adversity and has achieved the top of his field. He was also awarded the Presidential Medal of Freedom in 2008, the highest award a civilian can receive in our country. Dr. Carson and his wife have created a foundation to provide scholarships for those students with academic excellence and humanitarian qualities to help pay for their college.

His life story has been made into the television movie called *Gifted Hands*. He remains inspired by those students he helps through the Carson Scholars Fund. One scholarship recipient stated, "I probably should not be where I am. I went to Baltimore public schools. My father's in jail; my mother is dead. Statistically, I should not be here. I should be on parole somewhere or even dead. I never looked at it that way. I made it through."

> There are many foundations, started by many different folks, for many different reasons.

This student had read Dr. Carson's autobiography, also titled *Gifted Hands*, and said that is was "a relief to see someone who grew up in the city and didn't have a luxurious life but overcame it all," he said. "I love stories about underdogs, those who overcome adversity and do something." (Source: www.cnn.com/2009/HEALTH/02/02/carson.bio/index.html?iref=mpstoryview)

There are many foundations, started by many different folks, for many different reasons. And the criteria for money are varied as well. Want a sample of foundations? Here you go.

Here are just some of the foundations that give personal and business grants:

- ✔ Wheless Foundation, P.O. Box 1119, Shreveport, LA 71152

- ✔ Simon & Schwab Foundation, P.O. Box 1014, Columbus, GA 31902

- ✔ Coulter Foundation, P.O. Box 5247, Denver, CO 80217

✔ Thatcher Foundation, P.O. Box 1401, Pueblo, CO 81002

✔ Biddle Foundation, Inc., 61 Broadway, Room 2912, New York, NY 10006

✔ Avery-Fuller Children Center, 251 Kearney Street, No. 301, San Francisco, CA 94108

✔ Jane Nugent Cochems Trust, c/o Colorado National Bank of Denver, P.O. Box 5168, Denver, CO 80217

✔ Unocal Foundation, P.O. Box 7600, Los Angeles, CA 90051

✔ Wal-Mart Foundation, 702 Southwest 8th Street, Bentonville, AK 72716

✔ The Piton Foundation, 511 16th Street, Suite 700, Denver, CO 80202

✔ Frank R. Seaver Trust, 714 W. Olympic Boulevard, Los Angeles, CA 90015

✔ Earl B. Gilmore Foundation, 160 S. Fairfax Avenue, Los Angeles, CA 90036

✔ The Commonwealth Fund, One East 75th Street, New York, NY 10021-2692

✔ The Cullen Foundation, P.O. Box 1600, Houston, TX 77251

✔ The James Irvine Foundation, One Market Plaza, San Francisco, CA 94105

✔ William Penn Foundation, 1630 Locust Street, Philadelphia, PA 19103

✔ Blanchard Foundation, c/o Boston Sake, One Boston Place, Boston, MA 02106

✔ Xerox Foundation, P.O. Box 1600, Stamford, CT 06904

✔ Fairchild Industries, 20301 Century Boulevard, Germantown, MD 20874

✔ Charles and Els Bendheim Foundation, One Parker Plaza, Fort Lee, NJ 07024

✔ Blue Horizon Health & Welfare Trust, c/o Reid & Reige, Lakeville, CT 06039

✔ Broadcasters Foundation, Inc., 320 West 57th Street, New York, NY 10019

✔ Copley Fund, P.O. Box 696, Morrisville, VT 05661

✔ The Hawaii Foundation, 111 South King Street, P.O. Box 3170, Honolulu, HI 96802

✔ Inland Steel-Ryerson Foundation, 30 West Monroe Street, Chicago, IL 60603

✔ Northern Indiana Giving Program, 5265 Hohman Avenue, Hammond, IN 46320

✔ Cambridge Foundation, 99 Bishop Allan Drive, Cambridge, MA 02139

✔ Barker Foundation, P.O. Box 328, Nashua, NH 03301

✔ Morris Joseloff Foundation, Inc., 125 La Salee Rd, W. Hartford, CT 06107

✔ Deposit Guaranty Foundation, P.O. Box 1200, Jackson, MS 39201

✔ Haskin Foundation, 200 E. Broadway, Louisville, KY 40202

✔ The Dayton Foundation, 1395 Winters Bank Tower, Dayton, OH 45423

✔ Ford Motor Company, The American Road, Dearborn, MI 48121

✔ Bohen Foundation, 1716 Locust Street, Des Moines, IA 50303

✔ Yonkers Charitable Trust, 701 Walnut Street, Des Moines, IA 50306

✔ Miles Foundation, P.O. Box 40, Elkhart, IN 46515

✔ Ametek Foundation, 410 Park Avenue, New York, NY 10022

✔ Horace B. Packer Foundation, 61 Main Street, Wellsboro, PA 16901

✔ John B. Lynch Scholarship Fund, P.O. Box 4248, Wilmington, DE 19807

✔ Camden Home for Senior Citizens, 66 Washington Street, Camden, ME 04843

✔ The Clark Foundation, 30 Wall Street, New York, NY 10005

✔ Richard & Helen DeVos Foundation, 7154 Windy Hill, SE, Grand Rapids, MI 49506

✔ Muskegon County Foundation, Fraunthal Center, Suite 304, 407 W. Western Avenue, Muskegon, MI 49440

✔ The H&R Block Foundation, 4410 Main Street, Kansas City, MO 64111

✔ New Hampshire Fund, One South Street, P.O. Box 1335, Concord, NH 03302-1335

✔ The Shearwater Foundation, Inc., c/o Alexander Nixon, 423 West 43rd Street, New York, NY 10036

And these foundations give grants for medical and education help:

- ✔ The Fasken Foundation, 500 West Texas Avenue, Suite 1160, Midland, TX, 79701

- ✔ The Rosario Foundation, 100 Broadway Avenue, Carnegie, PA 15106-2421

- ✔ Orange Memorial Hospital Corporation, P.O. Box 396, Orange, TX 77630

- ✔ The Perpetual Benevolent Fund, c/o Bay Bank Middlesex, 300 Washington St., Newton, MA, 02158, Attn: Mrs. Kelly.

- ✔ The Bagby Foundation for Musical Arts, 501 5th Ave., New York, NY 10017

- ✔ Larabee Fund Association, c/o Connecticut National Bank, 777 Main St., Hartford, CT 06115

- ✔ Battistone Foundation, P.O. Box 3858, Santa Barbara, CA 93103

- ✔ Avery-Fuller Children Center, 251 Kearney St., San Francisco, CA 94108

- ✔ Vero Beach Foundation for the Elderly, c/o First National Bank, 255 S. County Road, Palm Beach, FL, 33480

- ✔ Smock Foundation, c/o Lincoln National Bank and Trust Co., P.O. Box 960, Fort Wayne, IN 46801

- ✔ Glifilin Memorial, Inc., W-555 First National Bank Building, St. Paul, MN, 55101

- ✔ Clarke Testamentary Trust/Fund Foundation, US National Bank of Oregon, P.O. Box 3168, Portland, OR, 97208

✔ Welsh Trust, P.O. Box 244, Walla Walla, WA 99362

(Source: members.tripod.com/promo_info/free/freecashgrants. htm)

Where else online can you find information on corporate giving? Yes, many corporations give grants. Visit foundationcenter.org/ getstarted/faqs/html/corporate_giving.html.

Foundation Directory

Foundation Directory Online, available on a subscription basis, allows you to perform online searches on nearly 100,000 foundations, corporate givers, and grant-making public charities.

> ...allows you to perform online searches on nearly 100,000 foundations, corporate givers, and grant-making public charities.

Use the terms "Company-sponsored foundation" or "Corporate giving program" from the "Type of Grant maker" index to find corporate funders. Corporate Giving Online, also available as a subscription database, provides access to close to 4,300 company-sponsored foundations and corporate-giving programs (the same grant makers are included in the above-mentioned Foundation Directory Online).

It also provides searchable profiles for over 3,600 companies with facts about business type, names and affiliations of officers and directors, and subsidiary names and locations to help you find local divisions and offices for a parent company.

Hoover's Online is a user-friendly tool for finding basic company information and news. The Company/Executive Info section of David Lamb's Prospect Research Page is an excellent collection of links that may prove useful in pinpointing information on a specific corporation's charitable giving interests.

The Internet Prospector's Reference Desk on Corporations is also a good starting point for researching companies. Click on the current newsletter or the archives for profiles of other web resources focusing on corporate giving.

Philanthropy News Digest (PND) is an online compendium of weekly news abstracts on foundations, corporate giving, and grants. Use the PND Archives to search past issues of the Philanthropy News Digest archive, dating back to January of 1995.

The Foundation Center's RFP Bulletin provides listings of Requests for Proposals (RFPs). Each listing provides a brief overview of a current funding opportunity offered by corporate funders and other grant-making organizations. You can subscribe for free to an e-mail version of this weekly posting.

Keep It Simple

Most foundations will have an application or form or certain requirements to apply for grants. In general, if you write a letter, a grant proposal, or complete an application, you need to write to the point and be brief.

Don't use flowery words and don't ask for more than one grant per letter. Foundations, in general, want to know:

A. Your plan.

B. State your needs.

C. Describe the individual or organization requesting the grant.

D. The financial potentials of your plan.

E. List supporters.

F. The total cost of your plan.

G. Describe how your needs will be met with their grant.

The foundation wants to see that their dollars will be wisely spent and help someone further their educational goals, artistic goals, business goals, etc.

Endless Opportunities

As I have said, there all kinds of grants for all kinds of purposes.

> There all kinds of grants for all kinds of purposes.

For example, let's look at the Bagby Foundation for Musical Arts. This foundation offers grants for those completing their graduate studies "who need additional specific coaching lessons to make their professional debut."

Those music students interested in this grant are required to write a short letter explaining the financial need and their talent. The grant is a "3–6 month musical study grant for promising young opera singers and classical musicians based on talent and need."

So if you know any young opera singers or classical musicians, let them know about the Bagby Foundation. The address is listed above in the list for education grants. The Bagby Foundation also offers several grants per year to elderly musicians.

The name "Perpetual Benevolent Fund" captured my attention. What does this foundation do? They support local area residents in need. Even a washing machine or refrigerator is an acceptable request for their aid. People helping people.

You may have heard that some foundations give grant awards only to nonprofit organizations. That is true. (You can form a nonprofit organization — that is always an option.) And many foundations give directly to individuals, like the Bagby Foundation and the Perpetual Benevolent folks.

What Are You Looking For?

Don't listen to the naysayers who say "normal people" cannot get grants. There are funders who support individuals, for:

- ✔ Research
- ✔ Scholarships
- ✔ Student Loans
- ✔ Fellowships
- ✔ Internships
- ✔ Residencies
- ✔ Book Authorship
- ✔ Schoolteacher Contests
- ✔ Artistic Works ... and on and on.

Many libraries carry the publication *Foundation Grants for Individuals*, by the Foundation Center. Check at your library.

Ask around in your local community. You may be surprised to find grant opportunities in your own backyard. Check in your town through local social service agencies, professional societies, trade consortiums, United Way offices, churches, art councils, civic clubs, or Chambers of Commerce, etc.

One of the free and easy ways to get anything? Just ask. Where to find examples of successful grant proposals? foundationcenter.org/getstarted/faqs/html/propsample.html. Don't overlook all the foundations and private sources that provide various funds. See: www.foundationcenter.org/getstarted/individuals/ or www.fundsnetservices.com/ or www.kn.pacbell.com/products/grants/locate.html.

Hundreds of possibilities are at your fingertips.

> Don't listen to the naysayers who say "normal people" cannot get grants.

More Free Money...

How can we find free money? Let me count the ways.

Big ways and small ways, it all adds up. Grants, tax credits, interest rate reductions ...

The internet and the telephone are two great tools in the free money quest. Most people have a phone. If not, borrow a friend's. Many people have a computer. If not, go to the library or use a friend's.

The official website of the federal government, USA.gov (http://www.usa.gov/), contains valuable information about all US government agencies. The first topic listed is Benefits and Grants. This link gives you lots of official information on grants, loans, financial aid and other benefits from the US government. You can even sign up to be notified when the benefit page is updated.

Govloans.gov (http://www.govloans.gov/) is your gateway to government loan information. This site directs you to the loan information that best meets your needs and is an excellent source for locating loans for children, agriculture, business, disaster relief, education, housing, veteran or just about anything for which you might need a loan.

Call and Click

Your fingers do the walking and the "heavy lifting" in this search for money. Make a few phone calls and see what can happen. Reducing your interest rate on a $9,000 credit card balance (the average American carries that much of a balance) from 20% to 10% can save you a thousand bucks!

> Your fingers do the walking and the "heavy lifting" in this search for money.

Calling your cable company and getting the best deal can save you hundreds! When it comes to car insurance, re-evaluate who drives and how far and how often. Can someone take public transportation? That can save you big bucks in lower insurance premiums, which will more than pay for the bus pass. And you don't have to fill up the car quite so much.

House insurance? One call to tell your agent that you have updated your smoke detectors or done something energy efficient can mean a couple hundred bucks back to you. Do you have a cell phone? Does anybody else in your house? Get on a shared plan. And watch the minutes and the texting charges. If you are text crazy, get the unlimited. If not, pay as you go might be cheaper. You can easily save hundreds per year by going with the shared plan. You also can save by calling your cell phone provider monthly and ask if there is a new plan at a lower cost or more minutes at the same cost. Cell phone providers frequently release new plans, but rarely contact current customers to inform them of possible savings. Ask your provider to evaluate your current plan and usage to make sure you are not over spending.

Hundreds of $, Hundreds of Ways

There are HUNDREDS of ways to get HUNDREDS of dollars into your hands.

Use all the help that is available to you. There is free help in so many unexpected places. Free childcare? Yes, there is Grandma and your sister. Not paying daycare saves you HUNDREDS!

Don't have relatives nearby? Swap child care with a neighbor.

There is also a nonprofit group called Angels in Waiting. They give love and medical needs to the foster children of this country. For some children with severe medical problems, their parents cannot cope. Angels in Waiting gives necessary medical care, but also that extra attention that can literally save the life of a child.

You may have heard of Angels in Waiting in passing during the media frenzy of the woman who gave birth to octuplets. Some nurses from this nonprofit group gave free care to the infants when they first went home.

For more information and to learn how nurses become foster parents to the severely medically needy children, see www.angelsin-waitingusa.org/aboutus.html.

Wheels

Interested in free transportation to work? Certain local and county programs offer this freebie. Erie County, New York, provides a "wheels to work" kind of thing. The loan can be used to repair your own car or to purchase one. This program has vehicles donated that you can choose from. Visit http://www.cfsbny.org/programs/.

Catholic Charities also has wheels programs. See www.catholic-charities.org. Also check out www.goodwill.org. Certain states have their own programs. For example, New Hampshire has a comprehensive program. It includes transportation and reimbursement for expenses.

The Child and Family Services agency also has wheels to work programs. You may be able to find one in your community. Many of these programs are to fix an existing car or to finance a loan on a newer reliable vehicle.

Every Penny...

Another way to keep track of free dollars is to write down every dollar you spend. When you see where it is going, you will be aware of many things you have been blowing your bucks on. Stop the little expenses and see how fast the free money adds up each week. It is found money!

- ✔ Use restaurant.com to find deals.
- ✔ Eat at home more often.
- ✔ Switch car insurance to a different company. It could mean hundreds more in your pocket.
- ✔ Use Coupons
- ✔ fatwallet.com
- ✔ couponchief.com
- ✔ coolsavings.com
- ✔ Pricegrabber.com
- ✔ smartaboutmoney.org

The Library and other "wacky" ideas

Now here's a crazy idea: use your library! Free books! Free newspapers! Free Internet! Free movies! Free music! Well, maybe they charge a quarter to check them out now. How long has it been since you've utilized the library in your community?

Restaurants and stores all have birthday clubs and email clubs. Join! You get free stuff and free food and discounts!

"Kids eat free on Tuesdays." If you go out to eat as a family, go on Tuesdays.

"Senior discount before 5 pm." Eat a little before 5 pm.

"Buy one entrée, get one free." Take advantage of advertised specials and unadvertised coupon deals, etc.

Go online to your favorite product websites. Many send free samples of hair care products, cleaning products, etc.

Food stamp recipients can plan on getting another $80 or so per month.

Food Stamps

The government's new spending plan has a lot of perks. Food stamp recipients can plan on getting another $80 or so per month. That is nice free money. As of March 2009, there is a record 31.8 million people receiving food stamps.

Another perk of the plan is the worker tax credit. Making work pay means you get $400 free money when you file your tax return. Each working spouse gets the $400. There are income limits: $75,000 for single, $150,000 married filing jointly. If you make more than $100,000 (and $200,000 married filing jointly), no credit.

If you fall in the right income range, it's a good credit. It's a refundable credit, which means that it wipes out your tax and if there is still credit left, you get it paid back as a refund. There is a one-time deal for those who don't work — people who are retired, people who are disabled, and people who don't work get a one-time credit of $250.

$250 in free money for all!

COBRA

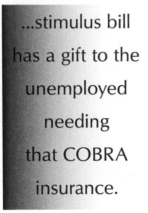

...stimulus bill has a gift to the unemployed needing that COBRA insurance.

Earlier in the book, I mentioned insurance and COBRA for those who end up unemployed. Because the economy is nuts and so many people are losing their jobs, this stimulus bill has a gift to the unemployed needing that COBRA insurance.

The government will pay 65% of the COBRA premiums for those who were laid off from their jobs between September 1, 2008, and December 31, 2009. The feds will pay that portion for nine months. That is a nice chunk of free money!

The income limits for that perk are generous. $125,000 for single and $250,000 if married filing jointly.

On that same train of unemployment, benefits paid to jobless workers (hmm, jobless workers? You know what I mean) will be $25 more every week. AND the first $2,400 in unemployment benefits will not be taxed for the 2009 tax return. AND unemployment benefits will run twenty weeks longer. AND if you live in a state that is deemed to be a high unemployment state (more than half, thirty states now), you get another thirteen weeks of benefits on top of that, too.

Ch-ching. Free money galore. Money to pay the bills.

TV

The government has a separate program due to the conversion of television to digital. These modern times do not mean that everyone has a TV that is ready to rock and roll with the new signal. I remember my grandmother had the little V-shaped antenna that sat on top of the television. Anyone else remember "rabbit ears"?

By June 12, 2009, all televisions stations will no longer broadcast analog. Digital broadcasting will be the way. To get your set ready to accept the new signal, you may need a converter box, if you have an old TV.

This transition means you either have to:

1. Have a TV that is digital ready.
2. Use cable or a satellite dish.
3. Convert your analog TV set to digital.

If you went with door #3, you will need a converter box. The government is issuing coupons worth $40 to offset the cost of the converter box. You can get two coupons per household.

How do you get your FREE $40? Easy. Go to www.dtv2009. gov and apply for your coupon. It will be sent via the mail. The coupon is not a piece of paper but a plastic card that looks like a gift card. You can use it at any store to buy the converter box.

The coupon card expires 90 days after it was mailed. To apply, all you do is enter your name and address in the online form. It's absolutely simple!

Do you have a small business? Need business cards or postcards or magnets to promote your business? You can get these items for FREE at www.vistaprint.com. All you pay is the shipping.

Turn on the Lights

A CFL bulb will last 10,000 hours compared to 1,000 hours for a traditional bulb.

Do you want FREE light bulbs? Many communities, including Los Angeles, have neighborhood programs. LA Dept of Water and Power gives every residential customer two free compact fluorescent light bulbs. These CFL bulbs save energy and thus save you money!

The press release states: "CFLs are one of the simplest and most effective energy savings tools available. One CFL can reduce an annual electric bill by $8 to $10. Just think of how much money you can save on electricity if you replaced every bulb in your home with a CFL! And, the savings continues because a CFL bulb will last 10,000 hours compared to 1,000 hours for a traditional bulb."

I don't know exactly how many light bulbs I have in my house, but more than ten and that would equate to a hundred bucks saved and free money back at me. I bet I have thirty light bulbs easily. That is $300!

For more info, see www.lacity.org/SAN/index.htm.

Utility Bills

There is also free help for those who need assistance with their utility bills. Go to www.hud.gov.

They make it easy in Phoenix, Arizona to get utility bills paid. There's an organization known as the Arizona Public Service (APS), and they have a program that helps low-income residents to pay their energy bills. That's right — you can get a discount of up to 40% off, if you qualify for it! Factoring in how much income your household makes each month, along with how much energy you use, the program makes paying your energy bills an absolute breeze. With those huge savings, you can use your money toward other things, like paying off credit card bills. Take a look at the APS site, which can be found at: www.aps.com. You can also call 1-800-582-5706 to find out more about eligibility requirements.

The Low Income Home Energy Assistance Program (LIHEAP) is a great place to go if you're looking for some funds to pay your energy bills. Run by the Division of Energy Assistance, the program is federally funded. The best part is that every year, money is distributed among all fifty states! That means that you should check to see what you can qualify for within your state. Get more information here: www.acf.hhs.gov/programs/liheap.

State by State by State...

There are so many programs, and we have tried to take the mystery out of it for you so you can see that a little search effort goes a long way. Once you start on this path, you will be amazed how much you discover.

To find your state housing authority office:
www.ncsha.org/section.cfm/4/39/187

To find your state attorney general:
    http://www.naag.org/

To find who is representing you in Congress:
    www.congress.org

Be Open to New Options

Writing your Congressman might seem crazy to you, but I don't think so. There are crazy ways of getting free money. My friend, Misha, gets $500 a month for driving her car! Seriously. She has an Infiniti SUV and it is now covered with decals for her employer, a company called jobing.com.

Her gas money and the $500 stipend are more than enough for Misha to be excited about this free money. Her company gets advertising everywhere she goes. It's a win-win. As Misha says, "You'd be a fool not to take advantage of it." (Misha's story was covered by CNN.com last year.)

There are opportunities out there for free money all the time. The more you make yourself aware and open, the more you will find.

Home is a Haven

It might not be $500/month, but home repair or home sprucing up items can be had for free. Besides driving around the neighborhood early to get your pick of the litter — the neighborhood trash — there are cheap and free ways to home improvement. How about free paint at the hardware and home store? If someone returns paint, a special mixed color, the store often cannot sell it and you can get it for free.

You can get carpet remnants for free or very cheap. Maybe you are at the furniture store. Ask if they have "damaged" items. Many times it is a scratch that does not show or a dresser that needs a simple drawer pull.

Many corporations have a charitable foundation and do things for the public.

Kids

The 2009 program allows millions of children to be eligible for free health insurance. See www.insurekidsnow.gov. Every state has its own rules. It can pay for doctor and dentist visits, meds, and hospital care. Call 1-800-KIDS-NOW for info on your state.

> Families receive up to thousands of dollars to pay their Child Care costs.

Some state programs available:

✔ Hawaii — www.coveringkids.com

✔ Connecticut — www.huskyhealth.com

Teenagers are covered, too. And working parents, these programs are for you! A short application form is all you need.

The Office of Family Assistance (OFA) runs the Temporary Assistance for Needy Families (TANF) program. Not only does the program provide free job training and education, it helps with locating grants that pay for Child Care. By contacting state agencies, it can find a program that is right for you. You can learn more at: www.acf.hhs.gov/programs/ofa/. Also, be sure to check out some other opportunities at: www.childcareaware.org or www.workfamily.org.

The Child Care and Development Block Grant (CCDBG) provides funds to assist with Child Care costs as well. The U.S. Department of Health and Human Services is responsible for heading this terrific organization. Every year, financial burden is eased, as families receive up to thousands of dollars to pay their Child Care costs. Parents are allowed to choose their own Child Care provider, as long as it is legally operating and it meets all state health and safety requirements. More information can be found at: www.naeyc.org/policy/federal/ccdbg.asp or www.nccic.org.

Preschool

Aside from Child Care, raising a child brings about a number of other considerations. Education is a fundamental piece of the puzzle, and it's something that we should never skimp on. Head Start exists to provide your child with free Pre-School! Geared toward providing low-income families with the tools to successfully enhance the development of their children, the program offers a variety of educational, social, and health services. Armed with the skills to go into kindergarten with confidence, children get a "head start" on the path toward success. You can't go wrong with this program. Go here to get more information: www2.acf.dhhs. gov/programs/hsb.

Car Repairs, Crime Victims

Victims of crime can get up to $10,000, even $25,000 in compensation.

You can get $500 for car repairs! If you live in New Hampshire and meet certain conditions. See www. dhhs.nh.gov. This is just one example!

Victims of crime can get up to $10,000, even $25,000 in

compensation through various state programs. The grants are made to states by the federal Office for Victims of Crime (OVC). Theft damage and property loss are not usually covered. See www.ojp. usdoj.gov/ovc.

Most funds come from two pools of money: victim compensation and victim assistance. For example, in Colorado, contact www. coloradocrimevictims.org. In Arizona, www.azvictims.com.

Money To Pay the Bills

Supplemental Security Income (SSI) is not Social Security. Elderly, disabled, blind and low-income folks get money to pay the bills! Cash to meet basic needs — food, shelter, and clothing. Over $600 per month for a single and $900 per month for a couple! The amounts are adjusted each year. See www.ssa.gov/ssi.

There are even some states out there that will take it a step further and actually *add* to the benefits that SSI is already giving! So what you initially receive may increase even more. Not only that, but if you qualify for SSI, you may also qualify for certain services within your state.

The Rural Housing Repair Loans and Grants can give you the free money or low cost loans to help you with improving your home. Through their program, you can potentially receive over $7,000 in free money! That's a lot of cash that you can put into your home, without having to worry about paying it back. This is a US Department of Agriculture program and you can get all the details, including more information about the application process, at: http://www.govbenefits.gov and http://www.rurdev. usda.gov/rhs/.

Pay for Parking!

Commuters, listen up! Yes, you can get government money to pay for your parking! Up to $230 per month! See irs.gov/pub/irs-pdf/p15b.pdf. (IRS Pub 15-B (2009) Page 20.) There is even a benefit if you commute by bicycle! Subject to rules, you can get $20 per month. C'mon, you gotta admit, that is amazing.

Food

The Emergency Food Assistance Program (TEFAP), commonly known as the food stamp program, is a great program to get help with emergency food assistance at no cost. The TEFAP is a federal program that helps supplement the diets of individuals and families. For information you can check out their website at: http://www.fns.usda.gov/fdd/programs/tefap. Managed by the US Department of Agriculture, the program contact information is: Headquarters Office, Food Distribution Division, FNS, USDA, Room 502, Park Office Center, 3101 Park Center Drive, Alexandria, VA 22302. For eligibility details and information on the application process, don't forget to check out: http://www.govbenefits.gov.

Clothing

What if you are looking for a job and need an outfit to wear to the interview, but don't have the money to buy new clothes? Instant savings happens when you get clothes for free! It may help you get the job, and the clothes are yours to keep. Most every state has such a program. Contact: www.dressforsuccess.org and www.bottomlesscloset.org.

Students

College students who qualify may be able to get a grant of up to $4,000 per year to pay their bills. Contact: www.ed.gov/about/

offices/list/fsa/index.html. Want to learn a foreign language? Get a fellowship grant to pay your tuition. Contact: www.ed.gov/about/offices/list/ope/iegps/index.html. You can get a grant for $28,000 to get your doctorate degree overseas and not have to repay it! Contact: www.ed.gov/programs/iegpsirs/index.html. There are hundreds of grants to help you go to school! Contact your school or state aid office or go to: www.studentaid.ed.gov.

Have you finished your degree and want to continue? Many grants and fellowships are available. See: http://www.aauw.org/fga/fellowships_grants/; www.grants.gov.; or look up grants in your field. Opportunities abound. For example, the National Institute of Health offers programs for medical and dental students (http://grants.nih.gov/grants/index.cfm).

You can also check out the Department of Education at: http://www.ed.gov/about/offices/list/ocfo/grants/grants.html.

Go For It!

Many grant applications can be done online. Follow the instructions, step by step. Different grants ask for different things. If you have questions, you can contact that agency directly. Most have help sections on their websites to guide you through the process.

For the federal government agency directory, you can contact: www.firstgov.gov or www.pueblo.gsa.gov/call or 1-880-FED-INFO. There is also a giant book, if you want paper to read. It's 2,400 pages. Detailed grant information is printed in the Catalog of Federal Domestic Assistance and is available for $75. You can order it from the US

> Many grant applications can be done online.

Government Bookstore at http://bookstore.gpo.gov/actions/GeneralSearch.do.

The IRS commissioner said on TV that many people are over-paying their taxes. We gotta quit paying too much!

As with most everything we have covered in this book, the steps to take are simple. Do step one, which is usually get the information. Step two is to act on it. That is the part I cannot do for you. But by golly, you will be so glad you did.

Even the IRS commissioner stated that getting the stimulus check was easy. And I quote:

"All it takes is a few simple steps, and the payment can be on its way. It's not too late to file, but the sooner people file, the faster they'll receive their money," said Doug Shulman, IRS Commissioner.

That one-time stimulus check of 2008 may be out of date now, but the sentiment is the same for just about all the free money techniques:

✔ Follow the simple steps.

✔ If you need help, ask. That means help as in money, and help as in paperwork.

✔ Just do it!

As in the words of the top dog at the IRS, the sooner you do it, the sooner you'll get the money.

Let me know what works for you.

Thanks for reading!

CHAPTER 24

Parting Words

$9 billion. That is New York alone. What am I talking about?

As I finish up this book, another news article was just given to me stating that New York state has $9 billion in unclaimed funds. Remember how we talked about the billions in unclaimed money and property? Remember how I said you need to check it out and see what share of it is yours? Remember how I said there are BILLIONS of dollars out there, with a name on it? All that needs to happen is the cash find its rightful owner.

Is that gonna happen? Or does the owner have to track down his cash? You bet. That is the way it works. (Source: www.theye-shivaworld.com/news/General+News/32374/New+York+Has+$9 B+and+It+Might+Be+Yours.html)

If you are East Coasters, try:

✔ New Yorkers — Visit www.osc.state.ny.us or call (800) 221-9311.

✔ New Jersey — Visit www.state.nj.us/treasury/taxation/ updiscl.shtml

✔ Connecticut — Visit www.ctbiglist.com

The money is there. Free money. For me, for you, your friends, your family, your co-workers …

It is there for the picking. And the time is ripe. The time is now.

I am looking forward to hearing your free money tips and testimonials. KT's Free Money newsletter has me excited already. Sign up! New sources of free money will be reported to you every month. Who knows what next month will bring?! More free money? You can bet on it!

I realize that more news articles and sources and information will cross my desk every day, but I have to finally let this book go. That is why we will stay in touch each and every month.

As for this book, it has been my pleasure. I hope it was yours, too. So…one more time, and I sincerely mean it, thank you for reading.

—*Kevin Trudeau*

State Agencies— Unclaimed Property

Alabama
State Treasury
Unclaimed Property Division
P.O. Box 302520
Montgomery, AL 36130-2520
Phone: (334) 242-7500
Fax: (334) 242-7592

Alaska
Department of Revenue
Treasury Division
Unclaimed Property Section
P.O. Box 110405
Juneau, AK 99811-0405
Phone: (907) 465-3726
Fax: (907) 465-2394

Arizona
Department of Revenue
Unclaimed Property Unit
P.O. Box 29026
Site Code 9026
Phoenix, AZ 85038-9026
Phone: (602) 364-0380
TDD: (800) 397-0256 statewide only

Arkansas
Unclaimed Property Division
Auditor of State
1400 W. 3rd St., Suite 100
Little Rock, AR 72201-1811
Phone: (501) 682-6030

California
State Controller
Division of Collections - Bureau of
Unclaimed Property
3301 C Street, Suite 712
P.O. Box 942850
Sacramento, CA 94250-5873
Phone: (916) 445-2636

Colorado
Unclaimed Property Division
1120 Lincoln Street
Suite 1004
Denver, CO 80203
Phone: (800) 825-2111

Connecticut
Unclaimed Property Division
Office of State Treasurer
55 Elm Street
Hartford, CT 06106
Phone: (800) 618-3404

Delaware
Bureau of Abandoned Property
P.O. Box 8931
Wilmington, DE 19899

District of Columbia
Office of Finance & Treasury
Unclaimed Property Unit
810 First Street NE, Room 401
Washington, DC 20002
Phone: (202) 442-8181

Florida
Department of Financial Services
Bureau of Unclaimed Property
P.O. Box 1910
Tallahassee, FL 32302-1910
Phone: (850) 410-9253 or (888)
258-2253 toll free within Florida

Georgia
Georgia Department of Revenue
Property Tax Division
4245 International Pkwy
Suite A
Hapeville, GA 30354-3918

Hawaii
Department of Budget and Finance
Unclaimed Property Program
P.O. Box 150
Honolulu, HI 96810-0150
Toll free:
Oahu residents—(808) 586-1589
Kauai residents—(808) 274-3141
Maui residents—(808) 984-2400
Hawaii residents—(808) 974-4000

Idaho
Idaho State Tax Commission
Unclaimed Property Section
P.O. Box 36
Boise, ID 83722-0410
Phone: (800) 972-7660

Illinois
Office of State Treasurer
Unclaimed Property Division
P.O. Box 19495
Springfield, IL 62794-9495
Phone: (217) 785-6998
Fax: (217) 557-9365

Indiana
Attorney General's Office
Unclaimed Property Division
402 W. Washington, Ste. C-531
Indianapolis, IN 46204
Phone: (800) 447-5598 or (317)
232-6348 Indianapolis area

Iowa
State Treasurer
The Great Iowa Treasure Hunt
Lucas State Office Building
321 East 12th Street
1st Floor
Des Moines, IA 50319
Phone: (515) 281-5367

Kansas
Unclaimed Property Division
900 Jackson Suite 201
Topeka, KS 66612-1235
Phone: (785) 296-3171

Kentucky
Unclaimed Property Division
Kentucky Department of Treasury
Suite 183, Capitol Annex
Frankfort, KY 40601

Louisiana
State Treasurer
Unclaimed Property Division
P.O. Box 91010
Baton Rouge, LA 70821
Phone: (225) 342-0010

Maine
State Treasurer's Office
Unclaimed Property Division
39 State House Station
111 Sewall Street, 3rd FL
Burton M. Cross Building
Augusta, ME 04333-0039
Phone: (207) 624-7477

Maryland
Unclaimed Property Unit
301 W. Preston Street
Baltimore, MD 21201-2385
Phone: (410) 767-1700 from
Baltimore area
Toll free: (800) 782-7383 from elsewhere in Maryland

Massachusetts
Abandoned Property Division
1 Ashburton Place, 12th Floor
Boston, MA 02108
Phone: (617) 367-0400
Toll free: (800) 647-2300

Michigan
Department of Treasury
Unclaimed Property Division
Lansing, MI 48922
Phone: (517) 373-3200
TTY: (517) 636-4999

Minnesota
Minnesota Department of
Commerce
Unclaimed Property Division
85 7th Place East, Suite 600
St. Paul, MN 55101-3165
Phone: (651) 296-2568
Toll free: (800) 925-5668 (MN only)
Fax: (651) 284-4108

Mississippi
Treasury Department
Unclaimed Property Division
P.O. Box 138
Jackson, MS 39205-0138
Phone: (601) 359-3600

Missouri
State Treasurer's Office
Unclaimed Property Section
P.O. Box 1004
Jefferson City, MO 65102
Phone: (573) 751-2411
Fax: (573) 751-9443

Montana
Department of Revenue
Unclaimed Property Division
Sam W. Mitchell Bldg.
125 N. Roberts, 3rd Floor
P.O. Box 5805
Helena, MT 59604-5805
Phone: (406) 444-6900
TDD: (406) 444-2830

Nebraska
Unclaimed Property Division
P.O. Box 94788
Lincoln, NE 68509
Phone: (402) 471-2455

Nevada
Office of the State Treasurer
Unclaimed Property Division
555 E Washington Avenue
Suite 4200
Las Vegas, NV 89101-1070
Phone: (702) 486-2025
Fax: (702) 486-2490

New Hampshire
Treasury Department
Unclaimed Property Division
25 Capitol Street, Room 205
Concord, NH 03301
Phone: (603) 271-2619
Toll free: (800) 791-0920 within
New Hampshire only

New Jersey
Department of the Treasury
Unclaimed Property
P.O. Box 214
Trenton, NJ 08695-0214

New Mexico
Taxation & Revenue Department
Unclaimed Property Division
P.O. Box 25123
Santa Fe, NM 87504-5123
Phone: (505) 476-1774

New York
State Comptroller
New York State Office of Unclaimed
Funds
110 State Street, 8th Floor
Albany, NY 12236
Phone: (518) 270-2200
Toll free: (800) 221-9311 within
New York State

North Carolina
Department of State Treasurer
Escheat & Unclaimed Property
325 North Salisbury Street
Raleigh, NC 27603-1385
Phone: (919) 508-5176
Fax: (919) 508-5167

North Dakota
State Land Department
Unclaimed Property Division
P.O. Box 5523
Bismarck, ND 58506-5523

Phone (701) 328-2800
Fax: (701) 328-3650

Ohio
Department of Commerce
Division of Unclaimed Funds
77 South High Street—20th floor
Columbus, OH 43266-0545
Phone: (614) 466-4433

Oklahoma
Oklahoma State Treasurer's Office
Unclaimed Property Division
4545 North Lincoln Boulevard,
Suite 106
Oklahoma City, OK 73105-3413

Oregon
Division of State Lands
Unclaimed Property Division
775 Summer Street NE Suite 100
Salem, OR 97301-1279
Phone: (503) 378-3805
Fax: (503) 378-4844

Pennsylvania
State Treasurer
Unclaimed Property Division
P.O. Box 1837
Harrisburg, PA 17105-1837

Rhode Island
Department of Treasury
Unclaimed Property Division
P.O. Box 1435
Providence, RI 02901-1435

South Carolina
Office of the State Treasurer
Unclaimed Property Division
P.O. Box 11778
Columbia, SC 29211-1778
Phone: (803) 734-2101

South Dakota
State Treasurer's Office
500 East Capitol Ave.
Pierre, SD 57501-5070
Phone: (605) 773-3379

Tennessee
Treasury Department
Unclaimed Property Division
Andrew Jackson Bldg., 10th Floor
500 Deaderick Street
Nashville, TN 37243-0242
Phone: (615) 253-5362

Texas
Texas Comptroller of Public
Accounts
Unclaimed Property Division
P.O. Box 12019
Austin, TX 78711-2019
Toll free: (800) 654-3463

Utah
State Treasurer's Office
Unclaimed Property Division
341 South Main St., 5th Floor
Salt Lake City, UT 84111
Phone: (801) 320-5360
Toll free: (888) 217-1203
Fax: (801) 533-4096

Vermont
State Treasurer's Office
Unclaimed Property Division
133 State Street
Montpelier, VT 05633-0001
Phone: (802) 828-2301
Toll free: (800) 642-3191 within
Vermont
Fax: (802) 828-2772

Virginia
Department of Treasury
Unclaimed Property Division
P.O. Box 2478
Richmond, VA 23218-2478
Phone: (804) 225-3156

Washington
Department of Revenue
Unclaimed Property Division
P.O. Box 47489
Olympia, WA 98504-7489
Phone: (360) 586-2736
Toll free: (800) 435-2429 within
Washington

West Virginia
Office of State Treasurer
One Players Club Drive
Charleston, WV 25311
Phone: (800) 642-8687
TDD: (304) 340-1598

Wisconsin
State Treasurer's Office
Unclaimed Property Division
P.O. Box 2114
Madison, WI 53701-2114

Wyoming
Office of the State Treasurer
Unclaimed Property Division
2515 Warren Avenue, Suite 502
Cheyenne, WY 82002
Phone: (307) 777-5590

NOTE: Each state agency has a website. You can search a state directly on the Internet or go to www.bankrate.com/brm/news/bank/19990420a.asp to click on the state to go to its website.

Debt Statute of Limitations

As always, this information was accurate to the best of our knowledge at time of printing. Always verify the most recent updates or ask a qualified professional if you have questions.

Use this chart to find the statute of limitations period for your state. Open-ended accounts are the category that credit card debt falls under and, as you can see, many states have just three years.

State	Oral Contracts	Written Contracts	Promissory Notes	Open-ended Accounts
AL	6	6	6	3
AR	5	5	5	3
AK	6	6	3	3
AZ	3	6	6	3
CA	2	4	4	4
CO	6	6	6	3
CT	3	6	6	6
DE	3	3	3	4
DC	3	3	3	3
FL	4	5	5	4

State	Oral Contracts	Written Contracts	Promissory Notes	Open-ended Accounts
GA	4	6	6	4
HI	6	6	6	6
IA	5	10	5	5
ID	4	5	5	4
IL	5	10	10	5
IN	6	10	10	6
KS	3	5	5	3
KY	5	15	15	5
LA	10	10	10	3
ME	6	6	6	6
MD	3	3	6	3
MA	6	6	6	6
MI	6	6	6	6
MN	6	6	6	6
MS	3	3	3	3
MO	5	10	10	5
MT	3	8	8	5
NC	3	3	5	4
ND	6	6	6	6
NE	4	5	5	4
NH	3	3	6	3
NJ	6	6	6	6
NM	4	6	6	4
NV	4	6	3	4
NY	6	6	6	6
OH	6	15	15	6
OK	3	5	5	3
OR	6	6	6	6
PA	4	6	4	6
RI	10	10	6	4
SC	3	3	3	3
SD	6	6	6	6
TN	6	4	6	6
TX	4	4	4	4

State	Oral Contracts	Written Contracts	Promissory Notes	Open-ended Accounts
UT	4	6	6	4
VA	3	6	6	3
VT	6	6	5	4
WA	3	6	6	3
WI	6	6	10	6
WV	5	15	6	4
WY	8	10	10	8

Source: poorcreditgenie.com/crstatutelim.html